Smart Steps
to
Smart Choices

Testing Your Business Idea

David H. Bangs, Jr.

UPSTART
PUBLISHING COMPANY
Specializing in Small Business Publishing
Chicago, Illinois

Publisher and Acquisitions Editor: Jere L. Calmes
Editorial Assistant: Rebecca Rasmussen
Production Manager: Karen Billipp
Cover Design: Joni Doherty
Cover and Interior Illustrations: Timothy Gibbons

Published by Upstart Publishing Company,
a division of Dearborn Publishing Group, Inc.

Author: David H. Bangs, Jr.

Creative Writer: Mary G. Shuter

Produced under the direction of: Richard O. Schafer, Ph.D.,Director, Distance Learning, Wisconsin Small Business Development Center, University of Wisconsin-Extension and Jeannette McDonald, DVM, Research Assistant

Content Advisors: Patricia Duetsch, Billie Gauthier, Joan Gillman, Kevin Jones, Jeanette McDonald, William Pinkovitz, Richard Schafer, and Fred Schmidt.

Contributions by: William Pinkovitz, Past Director; Erica McIntire, Director, Wisconsin Small Business Development Center, University of Wisconsin—Extension; Donald F. Hanna, Chancellor.

Library of Congress Cataloging-in-Publication Data
Bangs, David H.
    Smart steps to smart choices: testing your business idea/David H. Bangs, Jr.
      p.   cm.
    Includes index.
    ISBN: 1-57410-021-1
    1. Small business -- Planning. I. Title.
  HD62.7.B355 1996   95-39464
  658.4'012--dc20   CIP

Contents

Step 2: Your Business Idea: Does It Make Good Business Sense?

Step 3: Analyze Your Markets: Does Your Idea Make Market Sense?

Preface

I have found in my experiences writing educational materials that often the "fun" of learning stops somewhere around adulthood. For some unexplained reason, textbooks at this level tend to be very dry and straightforward. The philosophy often is, "there is something to learn, now read it."

If you have had an opportunity to glance through this book, you may have already noticed that it looks a little different—perhaps not the way you are accustomed to seeing a textbook look. Well, this has been done for a reason.

This book has been designed to help you enjoy your learning experience. Imagine this book as being that favorite teacher you once had who knew how to make learning enjoyable. That teacher who guided you and encouraged you to learn independently. As you read *Smart Steps to Smart Choices*, you are not going to be a passive learner—sitting back and listening as the author tells you what you need to know. You will be an active learner—able to experience learning for yourself. You are encouraged to take the information presented to you, interact with it, ask questions, and apply it to your own personal situation. Make use of the icons, the notes on the pages, the vocabulary help, the case study examples, and the workshops. All of these tools have been put in place to make learning interesting and meaningful for you.

I hope that you enjoy your educational experience with *Smart Steps to Smart Choices*.

Good luck and have fun!

—Mary G. Shuter

Acknowledgments

Many thanks and a great deal of appreciation goes to Shelly A. McLaughlin at the University of Wisconsin SBDC. She labored tirelessly to give this book its "look" and freshness.

We would also like to extend our gratitude to David F. Mills, Ed.D., District Director, SE District, University of Georgia and his business consultant Ronald Reaves; Dennis Gruell, Regional Director of the Connecticut Small Business Development Center; David Gay, Director of ISBDC, College of DuPage and two of his preventure clients; Jane McNamee, Assistant Director of Training and Public Relations, UTSA South Texas Border, SBDC Regional Office; Loretta DiCamillo, Director of CSI SBDC, College of Staten Island, New York; and Meredith Roat, Advisor, IL SBDC, Triton College for their helpful comments and suggestions.

Introduction

Have you ever thought about having your own business? Or, do you have an idea for a business but you're not sure it will work?

Yes?

Then *Smart Steps* is for you. This guide can help you think through your ideas and can help you answer questions you may have about starting up a business. Upon completion of the guide, you will be able to:

- Identify realistic and achievable business opportunities

- Evaluate those opportunities in terms of your resources, experiences, and interests

- Weed out those opportunities which do not have a readily accessible market

- Determine the financial feasibility of those opportunities which have passed the previous three hurdles

Here's How *Smart Steps* Works

This guide will lead you through four important steps in the process of deciding if small business ownership is for you. You will base your decisions on information that you learn from the guide as well as things you learn about yourself. Personal information will be acquired from Personal Workshops.

What Are Personal Workshops?

Personal Workshops are activities designed to help you work through the many decisions you will make as you prepare to run your own business. Personal Workshops are not tests, simply exercises to help you learn more about yourself and about small business ownership. You will find an additional copy of the workshops in the back of this guide.

You're Not Alone

On your journey through this guide, you will have the opportunity to meet seven entrepreneurs who will be working through the same four steps you will be taking. Follow their stories as you begin creating your own.

The following icons for six of the start-up entrepreneurs will be used to help make case study identification easier:

Meet

Ellen Redfern

Dave Campbell

Dennis Aney

Phillip Treleven

The Sandlers

Laura Cleminson

Create Your Own Personal Notebook

You will find it very helpful to take notes, jot down ideas, and collect information as you develop ideas for your business. Arrange your notes and clippings in a 3-ring binder, using *Smart Steps* and its Personal Workshops to provide the structure for your own "personalized notebook." You might place workshop pages, magazine clippings, and notes in such a binder. Use Post-Its™ to shuffle ideas more easily.

You will occasionally find a 3-ring binder icon located in the margin of a page. This icon is a reminder or a suggestion that you may want to use your 3-ring binder for the information given.

Margin Icons

Additional sources of information and points worth emphasizing are highlighted in the margins of this guide.

Meet case study entrepreneur, Constance Fisk. Usually you will find Constance's story in the margin of the page. Sometimes, however, you will find her completing Personal Workshops with you.

Call Out: Information worth pointing out or remembering is called to your attention.

Library Resources: Recommended reading found at your local library is noted throughout the guide.

Key Note: Notes, quotes, and noteworthy information is located in a Key Note box at the bottom of the page.

Key Word: Words and phrases that are considered business terms and are important to the understanding of the topic at hand are highlighted and defined in the Key Word glossary.

Step Back: Occasionally you will be asked to "Step Back" to an earlier step or workshop for purposes of review or to take a second look at material.

Information: This guide will provide you with pertinent business information as it relates to you on day-to-day matteris as well as for strategic plans for your business.

Tools: Personal Workshops are the tools you will use to help you test and analyze your business ideas and strategies.

 Learning: Running a business successfully involves you in ongoing learning. This learning will be selective and appropriate, fitting your business's needs and your skills, prior knowledge, experiences, and resources.

 Networking: You will not be alone as you make your business decisions. You will be given access to additional outside resources to contact for support and assistance.

How to Read This Book

Spend a few minutes previewing all of your material before you begin. Become familiar with the guide and the Personal Workshops. Begin formulating questions in your mind that you want answered as you complete the guide.

Read the guide and complete the materials from beginning to end. Although it might be tempting to skip over areas, it will be helpful to you if you complete each Step in its entirety.

Take advantage of the Personal Checklists located at the end of each Step as a means to monitor your progress.

Make this an Experience— Not Just a Book Reading

This book has been designed for you to learn the subject matter outside the classroom. The exercises and the forms that you find in this guide and its accompanying workbook encourage a different type of learning. You are no longer just reading a book. *You* will be actively involved in the process of learning what it takes to start your own business. This is *your* personal project. Enjoy!

Getting Started

Think you can or think you can't, either way you will be right.

—Henry Ford

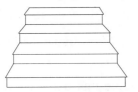

Getting Started

Success is more a function of consistent common sense
than it is of genius.

— An Wang founder of Wang Computers,
Boston Magazine, Dec. 1986

You have a great idea for a business. Perhaps you know a product that almost everyone needs, one you can improve, simplify, or sell for a lower price. Maybe you think there's room in your community for a new convenience store, a florist shop, or a computer repair service.

Maybe you have a feeling that you want to be in a business of your own but aren't quite sure what that business will be. **That's OK.**

Whatever your proposed business venture will be, you want to be sure it will work.

Now What?

How do you go about checking out that bright idea? How do you distinguish a real business opportunity, one that will work for you, from a business opportunity that won't ? What are the risks? Are you right for the business? Will there be customers? How will you finance your business?

Questions such as these are not only normal, they are signs that you are on the right track. If you don't have *any* qualms about taking on the risks and responsibilities of organizing and operating a business, something is wrong. Any enterprise that demands your commitment and long-term effort is worth your full attention.

Your business idea may be terrific, and pass all of the hurdles right off the bat. That's great; you can proceed forward with confidence. On the other

A Case To Follow

Constance Fisk has been an accomplished seamstress. She made much of her family's clothing herself, made gifts for friends and neighbors, and was used to a steady diet of compliments on her skill and creative abilities. One of her friends suggested that she start a business which would put her skills to work.

She thought about this and decided that since she'd enjoyed making wedding dresses, and liked working with brides, she'd open a bridal shop.

Now she began to worry about what she should do next. She had never been in a business of her own and had no business experience. What's the next step?

hand, you may find weaknesses in your idea, in which case you have a number of options.

- You might rethink the idea and find ways to make it stronger.

- You might want to postpone the idea—it may work next year but not just now.

- You might decide that being a small business owner isn't what you want after all.

That's OK, too.

The important thing is that these will be *your* decisions, based on a careful look at your business idea and how it will work out in practice. You bring experience and skills to this process, probably more than you realize. The primary requirement is that you use your common sense and don't kid yourself. The workshops within this guide have been designed to help you put *your* experience and knowledge to work in making the right business decisions for *you*. They provide an outline and some suggestions about how to proceed—but you are the one who will make it work.

Personal Workshop Preparation #1: What's In It for Me?

You probably have many questions that you would like to have answered as you work through your business ideas. Use this first Personal Workshop to help you prepare your questions.

Key Note

Small businesses are less risky than you might have been led to believe. Bruce Kirchoff of the New Jersey Institute of Technology found that after eight years 54 percent of start-ups survive in some form: 28 percent have the original owners, 26 percent have new owners. According to Kirchoff's study, only 18 percent of all start-ups fail with a loss to creditors. His studies are borne out by Paul Reynolds of Marquette University, who found that almost 80 percent of the start-ups he followed remained in business six years later.

Personal Workshop #1
What's In It for Me?

Smart Steps is designed to help you find answers to the many questions you will be asking as you develop a business idea. Use this workshop to help you identify those questions that are relevant to you. Place a check before those questions that you want answered as you complete this guide.

- ❏ How can I be sure that my decision to go into business makes sense for me?
- ❏ How can I find the right business for me?
- ❏ How will being in business affect my family?
- ❏ What kinds of people are successful in business ownership? Am I one of those?
- ❏ Do I have enough self-discipline and stick-to-itiveness to succeed?
- ❏ Should I consider a home-based business?
- ❏ Should I consider buying an existing business?
- ❏ Where can I get the business information and the help/advice I will need?
- ❏ Is there a right size business for me, large enough to pay off but small enough to manage?
- ❏ How can I get experience in the kind of business I want to own?
- ❏ When should I start my business?
- ❏ What's involved in making my business successful?
- ❏ Should I have employees or work solo?
- ❏ Should my business be wholesale, retail, service, or manufacturing?
- ❏ Who will my customers be?
- ❏ Will I have enough customers?
- ❏ Are there special risks in small business?
- ❏ Can I turn my hobby into a business?
- ❏ If currently working, can I afford to take time to start the business?
- ❏ Can I start a real business part-time?
- ❏ How much cash will it take me to start my business?
- ❏ How and where can I get financing?
- ❏ Do I need to know a lot of financial information to succeed?
- ❏ What would happen if I were to fail?
- ❏ _____
- ❏ _____

Here's What's In It for You

Will you get answers to your questions? YES! This guide will provide some answers for you. Others will be answered by you as you work through the materials. Upon completion of the guide and the accompanying workshops, you will be able to apply the following set of useful business skills to your business idea.

Information: Better business decisions are based on information that supplements and helps you evaluate your hunches and insights. This guide will help you identify the kinds of information you'll need. You will know when and how to get it efficiently. You will also know where to get help for those elusive bits of information that make the difference between winning and losing.

Tools: You will be given tools to help you analyze your business decisions. Workshops, checklists, and forms will help you answer questions such as: Is this a real business opportunity? Will it work? These tools provide a method to answer such questions before you invest your time and money.

Learning: Running a business successfully involves you in ongoing learning—but it will be selective and appropriate, fitting your business's needs and your skills, experience, and resources.

Networking: Going it alone leads to disaster. You will know when and how to seek outside support, advice and input.

Is your proposed business likely to succeed? The answer is— your business is *more* likely to succeed if it passes four sets of criteria: Does it make **Personal sense**? **Business sense**? **Marketing sense**? **Financial sense**?

Key Note

The collective experience of The Wisconsin Small Business Development Centers, based on thousands of interviews with would-be small business owners, shows that there is a straightforward pattern to follow. That pattern is reflected in this guide.

You will be able to provide answers to each of these questions by following the exercises and activities in *Smart Steps*. This process, which breaks the questions down into manageable steps, requires your thoughts and decisions. You will have to make the decision about going ahead. It can't be made for you.

Steps to Follow in this Guide

STEP 1
Does Your Business Idea Make Personal Sense for You?

Examine your business idea. What personal issues would a start-up pose for you? Your proposed business venture has to be right for you. You and your business have to fit. A business that would work for one person won't necessarily work for another. As an example, you might be able to start a restaurant successfully based on your experience in restaurants as a chef and manager, your savings, and your ability to attract start-up capital. Another person with a similar background might not be able to start her restaurant because she lacks access to capital, is unwilling to assume the risks normally involved in a new venture, or simply fears failure.

Ellen's Story
Ellen Redfern lost her job as a computer skills trainer with a government agency due to a reduction in force. Ellen found that her initial plan to sell similar computer training programs to mid-sized corporations became less and less appealing the more she looked into it. Did she have a good market? Yes. Did it make financial sense? Yes. Did it make sense for her? No—but this was a decision she didn't come to lightly. After spending many months researching her market and refining her business plan, Ellen came to an important realization. She realized that her idea simply did not make personal sense for her. Ellen determined that she did not want to be part of the corporate world.

Dave's Story
Dave Campbell made a better personal fit with his business dream of opening a wine & cheese store in an upscale tourist town. A former banker who had gone through some hard financial times, he wanted to combine his love for travel, wine and personal selling in a business of his own. His wine store is the result. He shows how hard work and grit pay off: he founded his store with the help of a friend willing to underwrite a modest line of credit for inventory and store renovations. The challenge of starting at the ground floor appealed to him, though he admits that it isn't for everyone. After several years, he's pulled back to 51 weeks a year of 60+ hour weeks.

Dennis's Story

Dennis Aney never really expected to start his own business. He had worked in the electronics industry for 24 years, almost all of which was spent in manufacturing management. Dennis was forced into "early retirement" when the plant in which he was working closed. One year after the closing, however, Dennis realized that he was anxious to get back to work. The plant's closing left a large pool of skilled electronics workers unemployed. Most of them were still living in the area and available for work. Dennis saw this as an opportunity to start his own business. He planned to manufacture printed circuit board assemblies on a contract basis for other manufacturers.

STEP 2
Does Your Idea Make Good Business Sense?

Can you explain your business idea clearly, in enough detail, so you can check out your assumptions? Is the concept sound? You want to be able to explain your idea: What are you going to sell? Who will buy your product or service? Why will they buy from you instead of from someone else? What will set your business apart from its rivals? Why will your business be successful? It helps to have more than one business idea to choose from (the first idea may not be the best you can come up with), so part of the work in explaining your idea is looking at other possibilities.

Phillip's Story

Phillip Treleven, president at GK Hall (the leading large-print publisher at the time), had a particularly clear business idea. His idea? Simple: find out what librarians, the primary market for large-print books, wished to have available for their large-print readers. Find out how the librarians wished to order. Pay attention to their ideas—and follow through! This made excellent business sense. There are 22,000 libraries which carry large-print books, millions of people of all ages who need large-print, and many publishers who are ignorant of large-print possibilities for their books.

Key Note

> A business idea "makes good business sense" if, in explaining the concept, a disinterested observer would be able to see that there is a ready market for your product or service, that you have the experience and networks to exploit the market, and that you can raise enough cash to start the business.

STEP 3
Does Your Idea Make Market Sense?

Analyze your markets. Who will your customers be? Can you win enough customers? Market analysis ("market" in this sense means those persons who might buy your product or service) provides the next set of tests. At the very least you want to make sure that there are indeed willing buyers out there, and enough room in the market for you to gain a foothold. This is easier if the industry you plan to enter is growing (industry analysis), but even in declining industries there will be niches which you might choose to work in.

Dennis's Story

Dennis knew the production end of the electronics business, but he knew that he had to become more well-rounded. Dennis began by researching the printed circuit board assemblies industry to look at trends and potential for growth. He found trade publications and other secondary research reports that showed that there had been strong growth in the industry during the previous few years, with 20 percent growth projected for each of the next two years and double-digit increases expected for the rest of the decade.

Dick and Ruth's Story

Dick and Ruth Sandler were intrigued by the thought of turning their rambling old house into a bed and breakfast business. Their market research showed that the local B&B market was almost saturated. They took another close look at their property, the market, and the competition and came to the conclusion that they would create a niche for themselves by specializing in functions: weddings, parties, and corporate retreats.

STEP 4
Does Your Business Idea Make Financial Sense?

Do the numbers add up? You need cash to make the business work. Think of a series of filters. Your business idea has done fine so far—though you may have had to rework it a few times, there's a positive fit with your values, ambitions, experience and resources. The idea itself can be explained

Key Note

Taco Bell and Frito-Lay were both started with under $500, provided by the founders' mothers.

and defended; it looks as if it has met the reality check of "good business sense." It passed the market filters: there are prospects out there, a competitive foothold. It makes *market* sense. Now the big question comes up: Will your business make *financial* sense for you?

Given a match between would-be owner and a range of small-business opportunities, it then becomes important to select one or two of the most apparently promising opportunities to concentrate on. Just as in love, don't get sold on the very first one. There are plenty of opportunities to pursue. You owe it to yourself to make a careful choice. The work involved in explaining what the business opportunity is will take you a long way towards making a sound decision about that business.

Laura's Story
Laura Cleminson, a young mother who designs and hopes to manufacture children's clothing, took another route. She realized that she couldn't afford to do everything at once, particularly since she was already employed full-time with her husband in another new venture. Her decision to go ahead on a part-time basis made good financial sense for her situation. She's growing as fast as she wants to—which is slowly and carefully—spending much of her time networking and meeting people in the clothing industry.

You Are Ready to Begin

The sequence of steps is important. If you want to start your own business, you can. If your motivation is strong enough, you will. As a rough generalization, small-business owners are smart, tough, energetic, resilient, persistent, and optimistic. They have to be. Owning and running a small business is hard work. If your personal characteristics don't match the business opportunity, chances of success are modest.

None of these businesses involves startling new ideas. Each represents common sense at work. The six entrepreneurs looked at their personal fit with

Key Note

> Ventures must also fit what the individual entrepreneur values and wants to do. Surviving the inevitable disappointments and near disasters one encounters on the rough road to success requires a passion for the chosen business. (Amar Bhide, "How Entrepreneurs Craft Strategies That Work," Harvard Business Review, March-April 1994, p. 156.)

their business idea, explained their ideas clearly before proceeding, took time to examine their markets, and made sure their resources wouldn't be gobbled up by too ambitious a start.

As you follow the four steps in this guide, you will sharpen and test your own business idea. The exercises, forms, checklists, suggested research, and other activities will help you.

Entrepreneurship, organizing and operating a business of your own, is a fascinating career. You can do it just as millions of others have. Good luck!

Step 1

Personal Issues

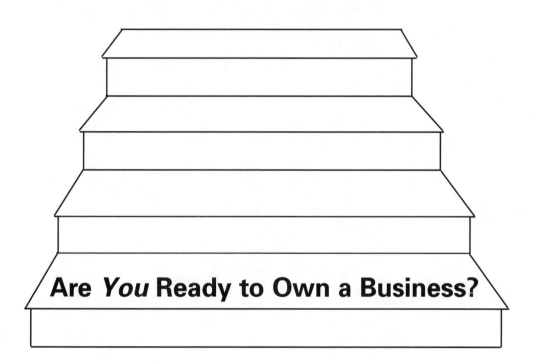

Are *You* Ready to Own a Business?

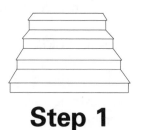

Step 1

Are *You* Ready to Own a Business?

"If your only passion in life is money, then maybe you should be in the arbitrage business. I love making good tea."

— Mo Siegel, Celestial Seasonings, Inc.,
Inc. Magazine, p. 49, Feb. 1992.

Do you have what it takes to succeed in small business?

When you complete Step 1 you will:

- Have an image of the business you want to be in
- Know what personal characteristics and business skills you will need to run a successful business
- Know where to get help in the areas you need it
- Become aware of the risks and rewards of owning your own business
- Have a more complete understanding of your personal financial status

Why Do People Start Businesses?

Starting Your Own Business is the American Dream

Want to exercise your skills and interests and make a difference? Try small business, as an employee or as an owner.

Want to be independent and make money? Then start a small business. Or buy one. Or buy a franchise. Or work in a business you can eventually buy. Or work in a small business to get an idea for a business of your own.

Want to stay in your home town, or live somewhere that's special to you? Small business provides the best chance to pick where you work and live.

Want job security? Small business ownership is much less risky than you may think.

The list of reasons to consider owning a small business goes on and on. Your motives may be to help others or to prove you can do something better than it's being done now—or a mixture. In fact your motives better be a mixture, because if you don't make a profit you won't be in business long, and if your sole motive is making money your chances of success plummet.

Why Did These People Want to Start a Business?

Ellen Redfern needed an income to replace the one she lost. She also wanted to be independent and use the computer and training skills she had developed over the years.

Dave Campbell wanted a business which coincided with his interests in travel and in fine wines. He turned his hobbies into a business which met his modest financial needs.

Dennis Aney was not ready for early retirement. He saw an opportunity to utilize his skills and the skills of other unemployed workers to start his own business.

Key Note

Do you think a person who was voted "least likely to succeed" in high school, doesn't know how to operate a computer, reads the National Enquirer and Cosmopolitan rather than the Wall Street Journal, went through four business failures and worked as a self-employed manufacturer's representative has much of a future?

No? Guess again.

Bob Levine, founder and CEO of Cabletron Systems Inc. is that person. But he is also competitive and persistent—which has made him a fortune and propelled Cabletron into the dominant force in its markets.

Phillip Treleven wanted to have a business of his own that would make life better for large-print readers—and librarians who serve the large-print market. He also was eager to move to the country, having suffered city life long enough.

 The Sandlers wanted to turn their white elephant home into a tax deduction and bring in some cash to maintain and upgrade it. Ruth wants to leave her current job and work full-time on getting the B&B started. Dick still has a regular job and will continue with it until their B&B is at least breaking even.

 Laura Cleminson wanted to build a substantial business, partly to show that she can and partly because she enjoys the designing challenge of creating a line of children's wear.

Table 1.1 reveals the reasons why people wanted to start their own businesses.

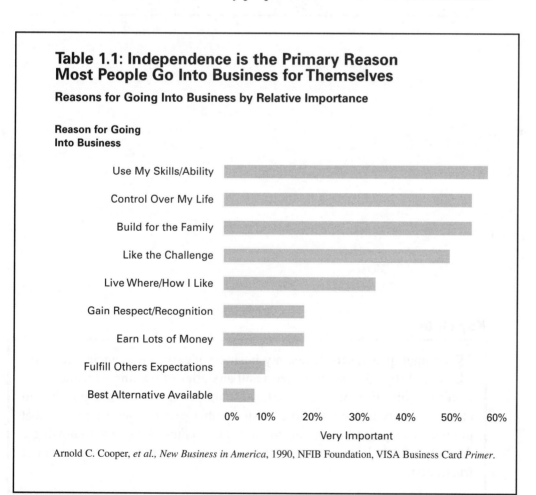

Table 1.1: Independence is the Primary Reason Most People Go Into Business for Themselves

Reasons for Going Into Business by Relative Importance

Reason for Going Into Business

Arnold C. Cooper, *et al., New Business in America*, 1990, NFIB Foundation, VISA Business Card *Primer*.

Personal Workshop Preparation #2:
Through the Keyhole

You will find it helpful to use the next Personal Workshop. This workshop encourages you to visualize and talk about your business ideas.

Personal Notes:

_____

_____

_____

_____

Key Note

The final question is "Does my business idea make financial sense for me?" Why take on the worries and anxieties of owning a business if it won't pay off? Few human activities are more frustrating than pouring all of your energy and cash into a business that doesn't quite make it, that joins the living dead of the businesses that sputter along never showing a decent profit. At least a company that dies fast won't provide you years of frustration.

Personal Workshop #2
Through the Keyhole

Have you ever said to yourself, "I can see myself running *that* business?"

Picture yourself in a business of your own. You might be making pottery, setting up a factory to produce salsa, distributing wooden furniture, running a fancy restaurant, or helping someone solve an interior design problem. Or whatever. Let your imagination loose.

Make your vision come alive. Talk about it, write about it, or draw it. What are you wearing? What are you doing? Are you in front of customers? Working alone? Working at home? Do you need a computer, a store, or a bulldozer?

You'll want to come back to this image again and again. It will probably change, maybe completely, as your ideas take firmer shape. But for now, just try to imagine what it will be like in your own business.

THE PURPOSE OF THIS WORKSHOP IS TO FORM AN IMAGE OF THE BUSINESS YOU WANT TO BE IN

Personal Workshop #2
Through the Keyhole

Have you ever said to yourself, "I can see myself running *that* business?"

Picture yourself in a business of your own. You might be making pottery, setting up a factory to produce salsa, distributing wooden furniture, running a fancy restaurant, or helping someone solve an interior design problem. Or whatever. Let your imagination loose.

Make your vision come alive. Talk about it, write about it, or draw it. What are you wearing? What are you doing? Are you in front of customers? Working alone? Working at home? Do you need a computer, a store, or a bulldozer?

You'll want to come back to this image again and again. It will probably change, maybe completely, as your ideas take firmer shape. But for now, just try to imagine what it will be like in your own business.

What Kinds of Persons Succeed in their Own Business? All Kinds.

If you are looking for a test that will tell you definitively whether or not you are up to the demands of small business ownership, don't bother. **There is no such test.** There are, though, some characteristics that successful small-business owners tend to share. Among these are self-discipline, stamina, persistence, and a willingness to adapt to the demands of the marketplace.

Take a moment to think about what success means *to you*. Not everyone thinks that making a lot of money equates with being successful. Some people feel that maintaining independence or pursuing a burning interest while still putting food on the table equals success. Proving that you can do something may be enough for you. You might find success in being able to arrange your work schedule around other interests. What matters is that you feel successful. While running a failing business won't make you feel successful—quite the opposite—being chained to a business you loathe won't either. Your aim is to profitably run the kind of business that accords with your values and interests.

A final word on this: Small-business ownership can be a rewarding, entertaining, exciting, and even exhilarating career. But it doesn't come without the burdens of stress, doubt, and anxiety. If you love what you do, it's well worth it. If you don't enjoy the responsibility and the necessary commitment to making your business work, then you will be better off working for someone else. That's a decision only you can make.

> *Experience has taught me that there is one chief reason why some people succeed and others fail. The difference is not one of knowing, but of doing. The successful man is not so superior in ability as in action. So far as success can be reduced to a formula, it consists of this: doing what you know you should do.*
>
> — Roger W. Babson, Financier, Educator, Entrepreneur

What Business Skills Will You Need to Succeed?

Take a look at Figure 1.1 on page 26. You can see that small business owners wear many hats. On any given day you will have to be the general manager: You will need planning, staffing, controlling, and directing skills. That's plenty to do—but you will also have to manage product development, marketing, sales, operations, personnel and finances. Even if you have employees who manage these functions you have to know enough about them to make sure the right things are being done.

Product and Service Development: Identify or develop products and/or services which will meet the needs of your chosen markets.

Marketing: Determine who your customers will be and how best to reach them.

Figure 1.1: The Many Hats a Small Business Owner May Have to Wear

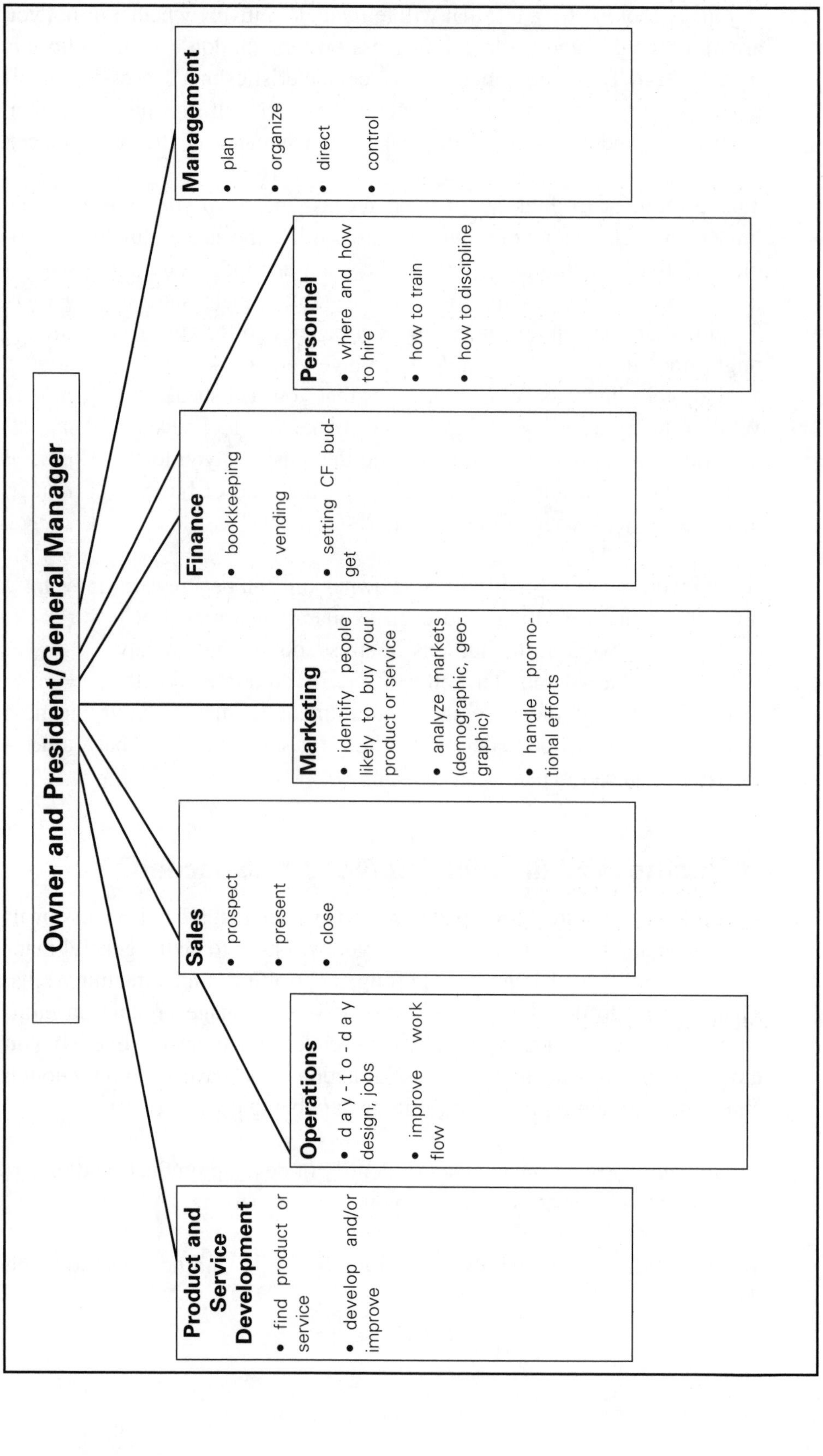

Owner and President/General Manager

Management
- plan
- organize
- direct
- control

Personnel
- where and how to hire
- how to train
- how to discipline

Finance
- bookkeeping
- vending
- setting CF budget

Marketing
- identify people likely to buy your product or service
- analyze markets (demographic, geographic)
- handle promotional efforts

Sales
- prospect
- present
- close

Operations
- day-to-day design, jobs
- improve work flow

Product and Service Development
- find product or service
- develop and/or improve

Sales: Get people to buy your product or service; make the sale.

Operations: Design, study, and improve day-to-day jobs—what people actually do during the day.

Personnel: Hire, train, and manage people (even a one-man band has a personnel manager: that person).

Finance: Make sure that money is available to meet current bills and finance growth of the business.

General Manager: Plan what the business will be, organize the business, direct the business (once it is going) by setting goals and timetables, and control the business by monitoring performance towards goals and objectives. Manage the managers (or self-management for solo act). AKA The Boss.

This may seem like an awful lot of work. Don't worry. You can do it—millions of others have. You will find, as you dig more deeply into these functions, that you are already exercising many of the skills that are required. You budget and control family finances, you organize and staff church suppers or baseball teams, you figure out how to do your own job better. These jobs and activities translate directly into business skills.

Personal Workshop Preparation #3: Ranking Skills

Take a look at the skills that are required of each manager. In the next Personal Workshop you will have an opportunity to identify the skills you have and the skills you need to improve.

Personal Notes:

_____

_____

_____

Remember Constance?

BRIDAL ELEGANCE

Constance Fisk wanted to make sure that she had the right set of skills to make her successful. She knew that she had the design and sewing skills (product & service development). She also knew that she had the personal sales skills that her shop would require. She acquired these skills when she worked as a clerk at a large department store. Constance also had the prior experience of selling bridal gowns out of her home.

Constance was less sure about the other aspects of her business.

• Would she have enough customers? Constance took a class offered by the Small Business Development Center that helped her develop marketing skills. Her counselor helped her do some market research which allayed her fears.

• She took a night course in book-keeping (six meetings spread out over six weeks) and read up on basic financing skills. She quickly became familiar with basic financial terminology and can now make good decisions about financial matters. She networked her way to a sympathetic accountant who provides her with the information she needs and explains what it means.

• Since she is her only employee she thought she could postpone acquiring personnel skills, at least for a while.

BRIDAL
ELEGANCE

Personal Workshop #3
Ranking Skills

Now that you know the many skills required for running a business, take a close look at yourself. Which hats could you wear comfortably? Which will need adjusting? Use the stairway below to rank your business skills placing your strongest areas at the bottom of the stairway and your weakest ones towards the top.

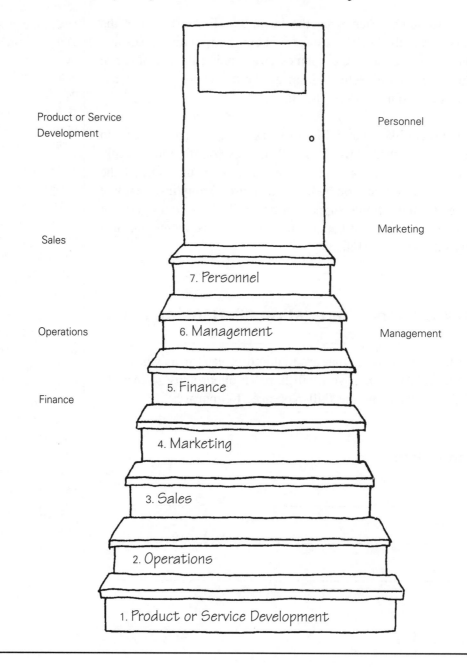

Product or Service Development

Sales

Operations

Finance

Personnel

Marketing

Management

7. Personnel

6. Management

5. Finance

4. Marketing

3. Sales

2. Operations

1. Product or Service Development

Personal Workshop #3
Ranking Skills

Now that you know the many skills required for running a business, take a close look at yourself. Which hats could you wear comfortably? Which will need adjusting? Use the stairway below to rank your business skills placing your strongest areas at the bottom of the stairway and your weakest ones towards the top.

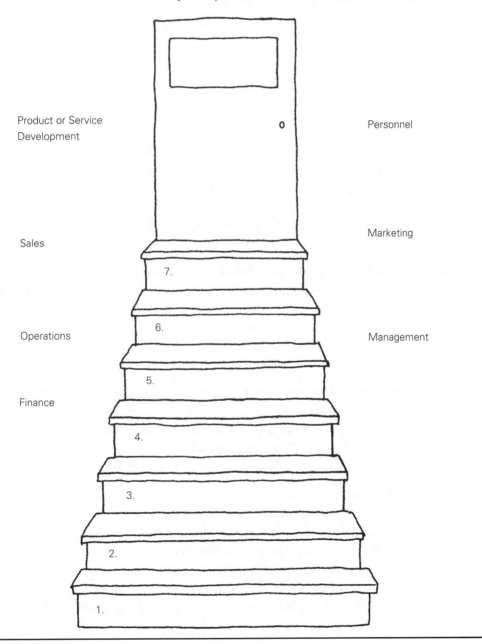

Where to Get Help

Once you have completed the Personal Workshop and have listed which skills are most important for you to acquire, where do you turn for help?

Small Business Development Centers (SBDCs) are sponsored by the Small Business Administration (SBA) in partnership with state and local governments, the educational community, and the private sector. They provide quality assistance, counseling, and training to prospective and existing small business owners. There are more than 800 service locations in 50 states and territories. Consult the phone directory to locate the SBDC nearest you.

Trade Associations. There are more than 80,000 local or regional trade associations. These are your best source for highly specific training and informational resources. Check in the *Small Business Sourcebook* for your business. See the listing that Constance Fisk used. It is a good example of the value of the *Small Business Sourcebook*.

Network with people who are in the same boat as you or are in business already. People who have been in business for a year or two will be close enough to their start-up experience to be sympathetic to you—and far enough along to know what pitfalls to look out for. How did they get the skills they needed? What do they recommend? They will be an excellent source of local information.

Bookstores and Libraries. Check *Books in Print* for titles that may cover your business. Every bookstore has this resource and will happily assist you. Your librarian can steer you to self-study books, textbooks, or other written material that can help you acquire skills. Local schools (including college level and vocational technical schools) keep their current catalog and course lists on file at the local library.

On-Line Services (America On-Line, CompuServe, Prodigy, and others) have small business forums, some of which are devoted to specific skills. They provide a place to ask questions, get information, learn what's going on in your kind of business, and a wide range of other information resources. This is an arena to be competent in no matter what your business will be.

Magazines provide a way to gain skills. *Inc.* and *In Business,* for example, have regular monthly columns and occasional, longer articles designed to help their readers learn how to manage better. Magazines such as *Home Office Computing* provide more specific how-tos: one issue (for example) had an article on overcoming feelings of isolation in a home-based business, another article called "The Small-Business Yellow Pages" included a helpful list of small business associations, and yet another article provided 14 sources of start-up cash.

Chambers of Commerce and Regional Business Associations sponsor workshops and seminars on very specific business skills. Start with your local chamber. They can steer you to local resources, including members who are willing to help new business owners learn the how-tos of running a successful business. Some chambers have formal programs set up to provide this kind of helpful linkage. They also keep up to date on business programs in their neighborhood.

The Small Business Administration has a raft of material covering basic business skills. Most of these are free or low cost. The SBA sponsors courses, workshops, and seminars on an ongoing basis. Consult the phone directory to locate the SBA office nearest you.

State Development Agencies are responsible for administering state economic development programs and policies. Located throughout the U.S. and Puerto Rico, these agencies provide consultation, technical assistance, and other services for industrial, commercial, and recreational expansion. With access to various funding programs, state development agencies work to promote the development of new businesses as well as retain existing businesses within the state.

Service Corps of Retired Executives (SCORE), sponsored by the U.S. Small Business Administration, provides free counseling and workshops for small businesses. There are over 500 SCORE chapters nationwide. For more information, contact the SBA office nearest you and ask about SCORE.

Personal Workshop Preparation #4: Getting Help

Where will you get help? Use the next Personal Workshop to identify and contact outside resources for self-improvement.

Note how Constance Fisk completed the form in this next workshop.

Personal Notes:

_____

_____

_____

_____

Personal Workshop #4
Getting Help

You have indicated in Personal Workshop #3 the skills you would like to acquire. Name at least two of those skills below. Then take action. How will you get help? Will you get a book from the library, attend a workshop, or make some phone calls? Use the resource list below to guide you as you plan to get help.

I Need Help With:	Marketing
I Will Contact These Sources	**Notes**
SBDC	Class offered—7:30 next Tues. p.m.
Bookstore	Jeff S. had a suggestion, call him for title!

I Need Help With:	Finance
I Will Contact These Sources	**Notes**
Local Campus	6 week course-begins next Wed. p.m.
Judy's accountant	444-3333 call for help

THE PURPOSE OF THIS WORKSHOP IS TO HELP YOU IDENTIFY AND CONTACT
OUTSIDE RESOURCES FOR PURPOSES OF SELF-IMPROVEMENT

Personal Workshop #4
Getting Help

You have indicated in Personal Workshop #3 the skills you would like to acquire.
Name at least two of those skills below. Then take action. How will you get help?
Will you get a book from the library, attend a workshop, or make some phone calls?
Use the resource list below to guide you as you plan to get help.

I Need Help With:
_____

I Will Contact These Sources   **Notes**

I Need Help With:
_____

I Will Contact These Sources   **Notes**

How Much Risk Are You Comfortable With?

Anyone starting a business will take risks. The question is how much risk are you willing to take on?

Career Risks

Career risks are straightforward. The time it takes to get a small business up and running could be spent in advancing yourself in a more traditional career. The time you take off to pursue your business idea may cost you a chance to advance if you were to return to that career—especially if your prior career was in a large business.

Family Risks

BRIDAL ELEGANCE

Constance didn't think of herself as a risk taker. When she looked objectively at the kinds of risk she would face and sorted them into risks she could do something about and those she would have to live with, she discovered that she was more of a risk taker than she had thought. The risks were not too bad after all.

Her main worry was that she would be skimping on her family obligations, so she discussed this with her husband and children. Together they worked out a schedule which met their concerns and hers—and assured her that their support was not grudging but enthusiastic.

Family and community activities such as being a den mother for the Cub Scouts, are high on Constance Fisk's list. She wants to make sure she has enough time to devote to both her business and her personal life. This will be most difficult during the Christmas holidays and spring seasons, when demand for her time peaks.

A supportive family is a huge help. A family that is sullen and unhappy about your venture makes it much harder to make that venture succeed.

The effort and worry that attend the birth of a new business can strain any relationship. A poor relationship won't be improved by the start-up experience. It won't make your family come together unless they are already predisposed to helping you achieve your dream. Your family needs to understand what the business will demand of you. This is a judgment that only you and your family can make.

The degree of personal and family involvement in small business is hard to appreciate beforehand. Successful small businesses are absorbing. You won't find ownership resulting in lots of carefree time off. Far from it. Small business owners take their businesses home with them, think constantly about their problems, and dream about them at night. This kind of commitment can cause all sorts of domestic difficulties, especially if the income the business generates is irregular. A supportive family can make the burdens of small business ownership lighter.

Psychological Risks

The level of your commitment to your business will have a very great effect on its success. This means that the business has to take precedence over many of your other interests, a factor to be considered carefully before you make the leap into ownership. If you value your free time, ownership may not be your best option. Similarly, if you want to be free to devote time to your family, or to civic or church affairs, or to pursue a hobby, or even to take vacations, think twice before committing yourself. If you work for someone else, at least you can (usually!) lay your burden down when you go home, look forward to time off, and have a pretty fair idea of what time is yours and what time is the business's.

The ability to discipline yourself and set priorities on your use of time is critically important. When you work for someone else, you receive orders—that is, the priorities are set for you. When you run your own business, you have to decide not only what to do and how to do it but also when to do it. And then follow through. One of the rudest surprises corporate refugees run into in small-business ownership is that they no longer have a structure to work within but instead must create their own structure. This is doubly difficult if they have been successful at working within corporate structures: the carrots and sticks that were used to motivate them as employees now have to be self-administered. This can be very disorienting and, in some cases, overwhelming.

Commitment, self-discipline, and success go together in other, more subtle ways. How you define success changes as you go along. As a student, success is defined in terms of academic and perhaps extracurricular performance. Failure is measured by the same people. As an employee, success usually involves getting pats on the back and promotions for doing the assigned job well. More pay or a year-end bonus and perks such as a company car or a corner office are viewed as inseparable from success. In both these cases, the rewards are conferred by some authority—a professor, a coach or director, a boss, an employer. But in your own business, you suddenly become your own rewarding authority—the professor, the coach, the boss, and the employer. Success in a small business sometimes means making the payroll, or acquiring capital, or simply surviving to face another economic crunch. Your payoffs become more internal, less overt. This can be confusing, and for some people the lack of feedback from an "objective" superior is profoundly upsetting. You not only have to reward yourself, you also have to discipline yourself. The guidelines are blurry.

The lines between you and your business can become hard to detect. One reason that there is no recipe for small business success may be that levels of personal involvement in the business vary so widely from one person to another. As an analogy, many people would like to be authors and reap the financial benefits of, say, Stephen King. But few are willing to invest the time and effort that being a successful author takes. The same applies to any field of human effort. Most small-business owners have a good idea of what it takes to achieve success. Few are willing to do what that success calls for.

Risks and Rewards

The most obvious risks and rewards come in pairs: the risk of going broke is offset by the possibility of making a lot of money. Being your own boss is offset by having your business and your markets run your life. The excitement of putting your ideas to the test is offset by the very real chance that your ideas won't stand the test of the market.

Personal Workshop Preparation #5: Risks and Rewards

Consider the risks you will face if you start a business of your own. List these risks on the next Personal Workshop. Then look over your list, asking yourself which risks are serious and which are not. See if you can eliminate or reduce an apparent risk by further study or developing a skill.

Consider also the rewards that you hope to gain from your business. List these as well. Do the prospective rewards outweigh the risks that you will be facing?

One way to guarantee objectivity in this process is to have someone close to you go through the same exercise. When you compare notes you will accomplish two things. First, you will be able to share your concerns and talk through ways of dealing with risk. Second, you will get a reality check on your anticipated rewards.

Personal Workshop #5
Risks & Rewards

Complete this workshop by listing as many risks and rewards as you can think of for the four categories listed. When you have completed your lists, review them. Which risks concern you the most? Think of ways you might be able to reduce those risks.

	Risks	Rewards
Career	Left security and complete insurance coverage	Being self-employed— I'll be my own boss
Family	Spending time away from my family— especially weekends	Family plans to work with me on weekends— teamwork!
Psychological	More worry and stress!	Feel great about myself. Positive self-esteem.
Financial	Cut in pay—initially	Hopefully business will be lucrative—more money in my pocket.

You may want to make a copy of this workshop and have someone close to you complete it for you. When you are done, compare your findings. Share your results.

THE PURPOSE OF THIS WORKSHOP IS TO WEIGH THE RISKS AND THE REWARDS OF SMALL BUSINESS OWNERSHIP

Personal Workshop #5
Risks & Rewards

Complete this workshop by listing as many risks and rewards as you can think of for the four categories listed. When you have completed your lists, review them. Which risks concern you the most? Think of ways you might be able to reduce those risks.

	Risks	Rewards
Career		
Family		
Psychological		
Financial		

You may want to make a copy of this workshop and have someone close to you complete it for you. When you are done, compare your findings. Share your results.

Lower Your Business Risks

If you already have a clear idea of what business you wish to start, the best way to lower your risks is to work for someone else in your kind of small business. Working for someone else is the best way to gain experience.

Do your best to find a job in your industry or in a closely related industry. Suppose, for instance, that you would like to examine the software business. You could go to work for a software developer, or a software distributor, or a software retailer (depending on which area most appeals to you) and plan to spend as long as it takes to learn about the industry. It may not be possible to find an exact match, but you can start by checking out your options.

There is no real substitute for paying these dues. Once you are in any business for a few months you will absorb information about it unconsciously: what's good about the business, what's a pain in the neck, what the usual problems and solutions are.

Your education is a part of your experience. So are your work experiences—and the sooner you can target those work experiences, the better.

Personal Financial Statements

Financial risks are measurable. You can look at your personal finances and make a good estimate as to how much you are willing or able to put at risk in your small business. Personal **financial statements** (both a balance sheet and an income statement) will be needed to support credit applications.

Key Word

Why should you fill out personal financial statements at this point? You want to have straight, supportable answers to three critically important questions:

1. How much money will you be able to put into your business? This comes from several sources. Cash and conversion of **assets** to cash should provide some start-up money; more money may come from using your assets to support a bank loan.

Key Word

2. What is your base-line living budget? Or: How much money do you have to have coming in from all sources to make ends meet?

3. Will your business generate enough money to meet your personal and business needs that aren't covered by other income sources? If the answer is no, then you need to re-examine your plans or find ways to

Key Word

lower your **expenditures.** Sometimes a part-time job or a working spouse makes all the difference—but you have to know what the numbers are to make the best decision for you.

Your financial statements reflect your position as of now. They become the basis for a projection of what your financial position will be like after your business is in operation. Your projected income, expenses, assets, and liabilities help you gauge the risk and the costs of going into business.

Personal Workshop Preparation #6: Financial Statements

Annual income twenty pounds, annual expenditure nineteen six. Result: happiness.

Annual income twenty pounds, annual expenditure twenty pounds ought and six. Result: misery

—Mr. Micawber in Charles Dickens' *David Copperfield*

Personal financial statements are familiar territory. You had to fill out a personal financial statement the last time you applied for credit. Even a credit card application calls for a personal financial statement. They are easy to fill out if you proceed patiently line-by-line.

In the next Personal Workshop you will have the opportunity to complete a personal financial statement. You will also find it helpful to view how case study entrepreneur, Constance Fisk, completed her financial statement.

THE PURPOSE OF THIS WORKSHOP IS TO HELP YOU COMPLETE A PERSONAL FINANCIAL STATEMENT

Personal Workshop #6
Financial Statements

Income

Look carefully at your current income, the income that you are used to living on. Your total income will probably go down somewhat during the first year of your business—but it may go down more than you expect if a significant part of your income is in the form of bonuses and commissions from your current job.

Annual Income	Amount ($)
Salary	
Bonuses & Commissions	
Rental Income	
Interest Income	
Dividend Income	
Capital Gains	
Partnership Income	
Other Investment Income	
Other Income (List)**	
Total Income	

Relying on a new small business as your major source of income is dangerous. It is highly unlikely that your new business will be able to support you in its early stages.

Expenditures

Your current expenditures reflect your current income level. As income goes down, some expenses go down too—income taxes, both state and federal, for example, are based on what you actually earn. Look at this list carefully to see where you can whittle unnecessary expenses, and also look at those expenses which may go up. If you have benefited from employer-paid health insurance, will you now have to seek new coverage? At what cost to you?

Annual Expenditures	Amount ($)
Home Mortgage/Rental Payments	
Taxes	
State/Federal Income	
Real Estate	
Other	
Insurance	
Health	
Home Owner's	
Car	
Life	
Car Payments	
Other Loan Payments	
Telephone	
Gas/Electric Utilities	
Waste Disposal	
Alimony/Child Support	
Educational Expenses	
Medical/Dental Expenses	
Car Expense	
Food	
At Home	
Away from Home	
Clothing	
Household Operations/Supplies	
Recreation and Entertainment	
Savings and Investments	
Cash Contributions	
Other Expenses	
Total Expenditures	

Expenditures (cash going out) are easier to control than income. If you expect your income to drop you will have to cut expenditures to make ends meet. Bankers will look closely at your personal expenses when making lending decisions. They won't be interested in financing a lifestyle based on more income than the business (plus other income sources) can generate.

Assets

Some assets can be used as **collateral** for loans or can be put into the business as part of your capital investment. Chairs and desks and bookcases, for example, can be used as office furniture; shop equipment from a hobby can be put to work making a product. This will vary from one business to another. Be as specific as you can with your list of personal property and "other assets."

Key Word

Assets	Amount ($)
Cash in the Bank (including money market accounts and CDs)	
Readily Marketable Securities	
Non-readily Marketable Securities	
Accounts and Notes Receivable	
Net Cash Surrender Value of Life Insurance	
Residential Real Estate	
Real Estate Investments	
Personal Property (Including Automobile)	
Other Assets (List:)	
A: Total Assets	

In Step 4 you will return to your personal financials as one source of money for your business, so be as specific as you can when filling out these forms.

Key Word

Liabilities

A list of your **liabilities** (what you owe) helps assess the strength of your collateral position. Assets you own free and clear are more likely to be acceptable to your banker than assets encumbered with debt. Note that some debts might be put on a different payment schedule, which in turn could lower your expenditures to a more comfortable level.

Liabilities	Amount($)
Notes Payable to the Bank	
Secured	
Unsecured	
Notes Payable to Others	
Secured	
Unsecured	
Accounts Payable (including credit cards)	
Margin Accounts	
Notes Due: Partnership	
Taxes Payable	
Mortgage Debt	
Life Insurance Loans	
Other Liabilities (list):	
Total Liabilities	
A: Total Assets	
B: Total Liabilities	
(A - B): Net Worth	
	$

Your Net Worth, what's left after subtracting liabilities from assets, will be a factor in credit decisions. A negative net worth is not a good way to start off in business: it means you owe more than you own, which, in turn, may scare off suppliers as well as bankers.

Constance wants to test her own credit and not rely on anyone else's, so she has not put her husband's income on the financial statements. She has included her share of the bills as she and her husband have worked them out—that is, she pays half of the mortgage, half of the property taxes, and her share of the living expenses. If she goes into her business full-time, she won't make her current salary of $12,300 per year. She may make more money; she may make less. At this stage she doesn't know.

Annual Income ($)	Amount
Salary (applicant)	$12,300
Bonuses & Commissions	
Rental Income	
Interest Income	300
Dividend Income	1,400
Capital Gains	
Partnership Income	
Other Investment Income	
Other Income (List)**	
Dress shop	5,200
Total Income	$19,200

Annual Expenditures		Amount ($)
Home Mortgage/Rental Payments		$3,200
Taxes	State/Federal Income	1,700
	Real Estate	2,200
	Other	450
Insurance		
	Health	0
	Home Owner's	400
	Car	400
	Life	0
Car Payments		1,620
Other Loan Payments		0
Telephone		360
Gas/Electric Utilities		600
Waste Disposal		120
Alimony/Child Support		0
Educational Expenses		0
Medical/Dental Expenses		1,200
Car Expense		0
Food	At Home	1,200
	Away from Home	300
Clothing		300
Household Operations/Supplies		200
Recreation and Entertainment		200
Savings and Investments		200
Cash Contributions		50
Other Expenses		50
Total Expenditures		$7,375

Constance has a net worth of $101,550, but much of this is not available. Her securities (a total of $11,500) represent savings for her children's education. She is not eager to touch this nest egg but it is available if she needs it. Her SEP/IRA would be taxed and penalized if she cashed it in. Constance also has $3,750 cash in the bank. She has $4,800 in equipment which she plans to put into her business. She has about $35,000 in **equity** in her home, which might represent a source of cash through a home equity loan or a second mortgage.

Assets	Amount ($)
Cash in the Bank (including money market accounts and CDs)	$3,750
Readily Marketable Securities	11,500
Non-readily Marketable Securities	
Accounts and Notes Receivable	
Net Cash Surrender Value of Life Insurance	
Residential Real Estate	
Real Estate Investments	100,000
Personal Property (Including Automobile)	50,000
Other Assets (List:)	
SEP/IRA	12,000
equipment	4,800
A: Total Assets	**$182,050**

Liabilities	Amount($)
Notes Payable to the Bank	
Secured	$3,100
Unsecured	
Notes Payable to Others	
Secured	
Unsecured	
Accounts Payable (including credit cards)	CURRENT
Margin Accounts	
Notes Due: Partnership	
Taxes Payable	3,200
Mortgage Debt	65,200
Life Insurance Loans	
Other Liabilities (list):	
car/loan	$9,000
A: Total Assets	182,050
B: Total Liabilities	80,500
(A – B) Net Worth	101,550

Personal Goals: Now and for the Future

Your *personal* goals are an important factor in making a decision about going into business. You may find that your business makes it hard for you to reach your goals and maintain your values.

Ask yourself: "What would I like to be doing five years from now?" In five years you might wish to open another store, or retire, or manage a much larger practice, or devote your time to research. Whatever. Use the five-year test to help understand what you'd like to do.

> "If you have a choice between making a business that's fun and fills a need and one that fills a need and isn't fun, you'd have to have a pretty compelling reason to choose the latter."
>
> —Joline Godfrey, Inc. Magazine, November 1993 p. 23.

If you're working towards a goal, the day-to-day frustrations of small-business life are easier to handle. The five year horizon also helps you define some benchmarks and a plan for attaining them. Maybe you want to be able to spend more time with your family, do community work, or some other non-business activity. Fine: The ability to pursue such goals through your own business is one of the most potent and satisfying motivators imaginable.

Personal Workshop Preparation #7: Personal Goals

You will complete a personal goals exercise in the next workshop. Establish your goals for this next year as well as for the next five years. As you go through the workshop, keep this question in mind: Will pursuing my business idea interfere with my personal goals?

> "The first two letters of the word goal spell GO."
>
> —George Eld

Personal Notes

_____

_____

_____

Key Note

Before you decide to risk your home, your retirement, or your children's education, stop and think about how long it took you to save that money.

Personal Workshop #7
Personal Goals

Write down your personal goals for the next year and for the next five years. Don't take a lot of time thinking about this. You can return to this workshop later and make changes. If you write down your goals you'll not only think about them more, you'll also take them more seriously.

Think of these goals as a work in progress. You'll develop other goals and interests and modify some of your initial goals. This first look gives you a basis on which to build.

My 5 Year Goals	Financial	Be debt free. Saving $ for college funds
	Family & Friends	Home time/help to lessen my work load—no holidays!
	Social & Community	Join the local Chamber of Commerce—get involved!
	Health & Fitness	Lose 15 lbs. and continue my exercise program
	Personal Development	More courses at the University—Who knows!?!
Goals for Next Year	Financial	Serve 2-3 weddings per month. Cover my expenses
	Family & Friends	Continue to be Doug's den leader for Scouts
	Social & Community	Continue to co-chair the local band shell fundraiser
	Health & Fitness	Join an exercise club and workout three times per week
	Personal Development	Take a 6 week course on finance

Personal Workshop #7
Personal Goals

Write down your personal goals for the next year and for the next five years. Don't take a lot of time thinking about this. You can return to this workshop later and make changes. If you write down your goals you'll not only think about them more, you'll also take them more seriously.

Think of these goals as a work in progress. You'll develop other goals and interests and modify some of your initial goals. This first look gives you a basis on which to build.

My 5 Year Goals	Financial
	Family & Friends
	Social & Community
	Health & Fitness
	Personal Development
Goals for Next Year	Financial
	Family & Friends
	Social & Community
	Health & Fitness
	Personal Development

You Have Completed Step 1

You have learned in Step 1 that all kinds of people are successful small-business owners. You can be one of them.

You've ranked the business skills you need to strengthen and learned to get help when you need it.

You've thought about how the main risk categories (career, family, psychological, and financial) will affect you.

You've examined your personal financial condition with an eye towards the changes that starting your business will bring: less income, lower expenses, some assets converted to cash or pledged as collateral.

You've listed your personal goals in order to get a handle on where conflicts may exist if you were to start a business.

This first step gets you off on the right foot. Successful small businesses aren't accidental. There is a right fit between the owner and the business— your goals and interests will be right for your business if you make it so. There is another important fit between your resources and the most appropriate size of your business. The more financial resources you have the greater the size range of your business. It doesn't "take money to make money" in the sense that you have to have a year's salary banked and own all your business assets free and clear before starting, but lack of capital is a small business killer. And most of that capital comes from you, one way or another.

You Can Go Forward to Step 2 with the Following

Financial statements to help you objectively look at your income needs and established net worth.

A learning schedule to help you address your needs in a planned way.

Resources for acquiring and fine tuning your business skills.

Use this checklist to monitor your progress thus far in this guide. Check off those things you have completed. You may want to go back and complete any activities that you missed.

Step 1
Personal Checklist

❏ Formed an image of the business I want to be in (Personal Workshop #2).

❏ Put together a 3-ring binder for my collection of notes and ideas

❏ Began to get help in the skill areas I have identified as my "weak spots" (Personal Workshops #3 and 4).

❏ Weighed the risks and rewards of owning my own business and discussed my concerns with someone close to me (Personal Workshop #5)

❏ Prepared my financial statement (Personal Workshop #6).

❏ Have completed a personal goals workshop to establish goals for this year as well as for 5 years from now (Personal Workshop #7).

Step 2

Your Business Idea

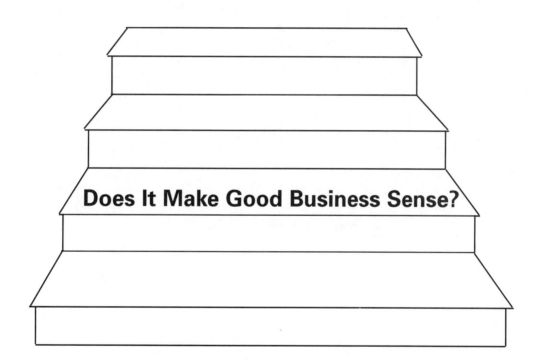

Does It Make Good Business Sense?

Step 2

Does It Make Good Business Sense?

Simplicity is indeed often the sign of truth and a criterion of beauty.

–Mahlon Hoagland,
Toward the Habit of Truth

All successful businesses (e.g., businesses that are profitable enough to stay in business and meet the owner's financial expectations) are built on three building blocks: Concept, Customers, and Cash. You need a good business idea, a receptive market, and enough cash to get the business off on the right foot for your business to prosper.

Your Concept, your business idea, has to be sound and make good business sense. Step 2 will help you determine if it does. Begin by explaining what your idea is. If your idea is a good one, you will be able to explain it clearly—in fact, the better the idea, the easier it will be to explain it to investors, suppliers, employees, and other interested parties. An idea that is difficult to explain will, more often than not, be an idea with serious problems.

When you complete Step 2, you will:

- Understand how to develop business ideas
- Know what goes into a clear business description
- Be able to specify what your competitive edge will be
- Distinguish a good idea from a bad one
- Explain why your business idea will be successful

Where Do Business Ideas Come From?

According to *Inc.* (January 1993, pp. 72 ff.), great ideas come from peer groups, mentors, visits to other companies, your own personalized notebook in which you put clippings and jot down notes and thoughts as they occur to you, industry conferences, competitors, customers, and company suggestion boxes and databases.

Many business ideas will come from your own experience and observations: reading, traveling, and in general, keeping your eyes open for businesses which you think you might be interested in. There are books and magazines which offer lists of businesses, newspaper articles about interesting or profitable businesses, and television and radio business shows which focus on new business opportunities. Keep track of those business ideas that most appeal to you.

It is important that you choose from more than one potential business, in part to protect yourself from a hasty decision. The more you look around, think about possible businesses to enter, the more ideas you will generate. One of these new ideas could be the one you have been looking for.

Key Note

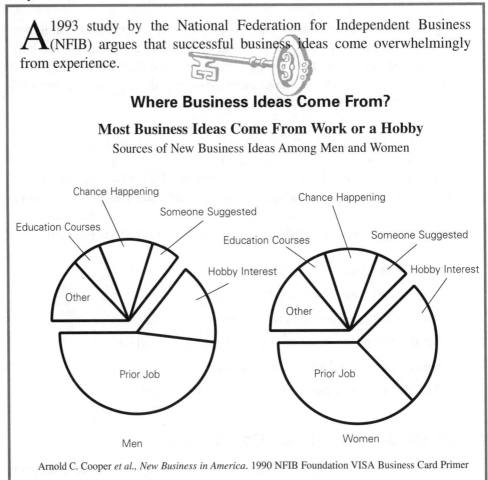

A 1993 study by the National Federation for Independent Business (NFIB) argues that successful business ideas come overwhelmingly from experience.

Where Business Ideas Come From?

Most Business Ideas Come From Work or a Hobby

Sources of New Business Ideas Among Men and Women

Chance Happening
Someone Suggested
Education Courses
Hobby Interest
Other
Prior Job

Men

Chance Happening
Someone Suggested
Education Courses
Hobby Interest
Other
Prior Job

Women

Arnold C. Cooper *et al.*, *New Business in America*. 1990 NFIB Foundation VISA Business Card Primer

Prior Jobs

Over 50 percent of men and over 26 percent of women derive their business ideas from prior experience in business. This should come as no surprise. If you are active in a profession or business, you will become aware of the opportunities in your field sooner than someone unfamiliar with the business. For example, it is not surprising that pharmaceutical companies tend to be started by doctors, or manufacturing companies by engineers. Cabletron was started by two cable salesmen whose customers demanded something that their cable company didn't provide. Paychex was started by Tom Golisano, whose experience was with ADP, the biggest payroll service provider. ADP refused to go after what he felt would be a profitable market niche, small business—so he started a company to exploit his insight. Golisano created the second-largest payroll service provider in the U.S.

There is a danger here. If you have been laid off because your industry is shrinking, starting a business in the same industry might be chancy. It is tempting to go with the business you know–but not always smart.

Phillip Treleven wouldn't have been likely to start his large-print press if he hadn't been experienced in that industry. His years as president of GK Hall, at that time the leading large-print press, prepared him to spot a major market opportunity.

Ellen Redfern's initial idea sprang directly from her experience as a computer skills trainer. She spent over twenty years helping people become comfortable using computers in areas as diverse as word processing, CAD/CAE and preparing presentations. She ascertained, through reading and telephone research, that computer literacy programs were in growing demand in private industry. Since she had made a career of developing and leading similar programs for the government, she knew that she had the technical skills and would be able to transfer those skills to a corporate market. She had kept in touch with several of her students who had gone into large corporations. These people would (she hoped) provide her with referrals and introductions to help her market her training service.

Hobbies or Special Interests

Fifteen percent of men and 25 percent of women business owners got started by extending a hobby or special interest into a career. Again, this is not surprising. Successful businesses tend to reflect the owner's interests, and one sure gauge of an interest is the willingness to spend time pursuing it.

An avid scuba diver, for example, might open a business that provides scuba gear and training to other enthusiasts. Apple Computer was started in the proverbial garage by two computer hobbyists, Steve Jobs and Steve Wozniak.

Dave Campbell's idea for a specialized wine store came from his hobbies. He likes to travel (who doesn't?), enjoys fine wines and the mystique surrounding them. He's an oenophile: a wine-lover who would subscribe to wine magazines and go to tastings no matter what else was going on in his life.

Laura Cleminson's ideas about designing and marketing children's clothing reflect her special interests. She has strong convictions about her products from being a mother, a part-time designer, and a consumer. Her interests in mothers and children's issues is long-standing; accordingly, she plans to use some of her earnings to help these causes.

Other Sources of Business Ideas

Education, chance, "someone suggested it," and "other" accounted for the rest of the business owners surveyed in the NFIB study. As Thomas Edison remarked, "fortune favors the prepared mind." Your education may lead to a great business idea—think of the case studies you read, classroom discussions about different businesses, or visiting lecturers talking about their business progress. Any of these might spark a viable business idea; your experience and skills are the tinder. Chance, or luck, or a friend's suggestion that you might consider this or that business, or "it just came to me" have been cited as sources, but you'd be silly to rely on such good fortune. Better buy a lottery ticket. At least that way you only risk losing a dollar.

The Sandlers owned a home that could be put to use as a B&B—and saw how they could put its covered porches, garden, and pool area to use for weddings and other sizable events.

Personal Workshop Preparation #8:
My Do and Don't List

If you think that your list of business ideas is too short or too confining, pay a visit to your library and look through copies of magazines such as *Inc., Entrepreneur, In Business,* and *Business Week.* Leaf through general business magazines such as *Forbes* and *Fortune.* Check the business sections of big-city newspapers and the *Wall Street Journal.* Ask the librarian about other sources—books, databases, "special reports," and monographs.

Familiar territory, such as hobbies and prior jobs, may also be excellent sources for ideas. Business ideas are often extensions of hobbies or prior career experiences.

Use the next Personal Workshop to help you begin to narrow your list of business ideas. Select those ideas which you like and delete those ideas you know will not work for you.

• List five businesses you would like to enter. Let your imagination loose: If you think it would be fun to run a theater, or have a store which is a community gathering place, or turn your hobby into a business, fine. Your aim here is to continue the process of understanding what you would like to do.

• List five businesses you know you don't want to enter. Sometimes knowing what you definitely do not want to do will help you find out what you do want to do.

• If you already have an idea, think of related businesses that could meet your goals if your first choice does not work out.

Personal Notes

_____

_____

_____

Key Note

While at your library or local Small Business Development Center, look for copies of *The Small Business Sourcebook.* This is a two-volume set steering you to almost unlimited information on the small business of your choice. While not every small business will be listed (Children's Clothing: Design and Manufacture is not), most will be. *The Small Business Sourcebook* provides information on trade associations, consultants, seminars, publications, and periodicals. It's a don't-miss tool. As examples, there are six pages devoted to wine & cheese stores, twenty pages to publishing, five pages to consulting. And that's just the beginning.

Personal Workshop #8
My Do and Don't List

What business do you see yourself in? What business don't you want to be in? List five businesses for each heading listed below. When you have completed your lists, look closely at your Do list. This list will help guide you as you continue to explore business ideas that are suitable for you.

Businesses

I DO Want to Be In: **I DON'T Want to Be In:**

1. _____   1. _____

   _____   _____

2. _____   2. _____

   _____   _____

3. _____   3. _____

   _____   _____

4. _____   4. _____

   _____   _____

5. _____   5. _____

   _____   _____

What Are the Opportunities?

There are plenty of small business opportunities out there. In fact, in this era of rapid technological change and economic shifts, there have never been more opportunities for small business owners.

Changing Employment Patterns

Downsizing, re-engineering, and outsourcing are having dramatic impacts on employment patterns. Middle management has been hard hit, as have untrained workers. In the former case, extensive use of computer and communication technologies has made it possible for small teams to accomplish what formerly required numerous well-educated and well-trained personnel to accomplish. In the latter case, robotics and more efficient work planning (including such modes of management as just-in-time inventory control) have made it possible for fewer people to produce far more than was formerly possible. While the consequent improvements in productivity benefit society as a whole, the effects on assembly-line workers have been close to catastrophic.

A Service-Based Economy

The shift from a largely manufacturing to an increasingly service-based economy has created a new wave of service-based businesses. These aren't confined to hamburger flipping. Financial services, paramedical services, communications services, and temporary employee services all provide interesting and lucrative business opportunities.

Technological Changes

Rapid advances in technology provide boundless opportunities for new information-based businesses. Increasing numbers of people are working at home, either for a corporation or for themselves. Many physically challenged people now have the opportunity to earn a living thanks to the computer/fax/modem.

The Green Revolution

Heightened environmental awareness and ecological concerns create business opportunities. Just coping with the paperwork and the flood of infor-

Key Note

John Chuang started MacTemps in Cambridge, Massachusetts, a $40,000,000 temporary employment firm with 6,000 temporary workers. His firm takes advantage of a niche market: temporary workers with excellent computer skills. This niche was created by the trend of large employers to pare down staff, then hire temps to meet peak work loads.

mation concerning environmentally sensitive materials has made more than one fortune. And as environmental concerns grow, so will the opportunities to manage and re-use and recycle more and more things that are currently tossed into landfills. Social concerns over polluted air and the impact of endless traffic jams on commuters' stress as well as communities' health have already led to an explosion in work-at-home arrangements. It is estimated that up to 44 million persons currently work at home more than one day a week. Think of the ways that this huge market might be served.

When Ellen Redfern decided that she didn't want to continue in the computer training area, she looked for other business ideas. The one she decided to go forward with involves "green" (environmentally safe) products for the home: everything from earthworms to compost garbage under the sink to biodegradable diapers. While she still is wrestling with how to create a business from this array of products (catalog sales? "green" parties? a store?), she thinks it's a good direction for her to follow.

Home Businesses/Telecommuting

The ability to work at home, connected to the rest of the world by phone, fax and modem, has created a huge market for goods and services targeted at persons with home-based businesses. This market includes telecommuters, persons who work for someone else but work at home one or more days a week. There are magazines and newsletters, electronic bulletin boards and computer-related services, home office furniture and many more products which make working at home easier and less lonely. And this market is growing rapidly: In 1994 Link Resources' National Work-At-Home Survey discovered 4,200,000 new home-based businesses.

An Older Population

An increasingly healthy population creates a demand for more leisure and travel possibilities. Different kinds of health care and housing for this population will be developed. It's inevitable: the need is there, and where there is need there is opportunity.

The Challenge of the Inner Cities

Perhaps the largest set of challenges we face as a nation of entrepreneurs will be how to involve inner-city and other underprivileged youth in America's business. Training and education that utilize new technologies such as interactive CD-roms and other patient tutors could make effective literacy available to all, no matter what their background. The payoff for solving these complex problems will be immense.

International Trade

Importing and exporting are increasingly becoming opportunities for small businesses of all kinds. Travel and language aren't barriers these days. English is effectively the global language, for both business and science, of the 21st century. Air travel and allied freight services make moving people and things easy—and the Internet and other electronic pathways provide instantaneous communication worldwide. The possibilities for small business are staggering.

Privatization

As governments from the local level on up privatize basic services, small business opportunities arise on a broad basis. These services include education, police and security, trash hauling, providing medical and health-related services, transportation and many ancillary services such as secretarial and keypunching services. If it is more cost-effective for a municipality to farm a service out to the private sector, you can bet a case will be strongly made for farming that service out.

Find Your Opportunity

The number of opportunities keeps expanding. Wherever there is a need and a market that can be reached and served, there's a potential business. It doesn't matter whether it's in retail, wholesale, service, or manufacturing. Find a need and fill it.

In sum, the first problem you face as an entrepreneur isn't a lack of opportunities. Quite the reverse. There are so many opportunities out there, from part-time income supplementing businesses to budding Fortune 500 firms, that the real problem is finding the right opportunity for you and your resources, interests, skills, and experience. Ideas for new or improved businesses—or even continuing a prospering business—are everywhere.

Key Note

LTC (for "long-term care") is a start-up which plans to organize the delivery of many medical services which will be needed by our aging population. Founded by a team with extensive experience in diagnostic laboratories, they discerned a growing need for high-level, inexpensive, timely services for nursing homes, at-home care, and clinics which focus on the medical needs of the elderly.

Business ideas that survive conscious scrutiny and outlast competing ideas beat hunches and flashes of insight almost every time. If you are serious about getting into a business of your own, your 3-ring binder should be your constant companion. Keep notes as you go along. The end results will be better than if you rely on your memory.

You can deliberately set out to find a successful business that you can imitate. If a business concept works somewhere else, the reasoning goes, maybe it will work here. Gourmet coffee shops that serve up cappuccino and caffe latte in pleasant surroundings are a good example. The concept began in Seattle and was quickly and successfully picked up by imitators from coast to coast.

However you come up with a business idea, write it down. The 3-ring binder suggestion is not made lightly. Memories are too fallible and ideas too elusive and valuable to risk losing. Your 3-ring binder remains the most useful tool for your research. Over time, your written reminders will help you clarify business ideas, help you determine how to best match your personal goals to your business goals, and eventually lead you to the best business opportunity for you, given your interests and resources.

Personal Workshop Preparation #9: Visualizing My Business

Now: What business are you going to be in? You can always change your mind, but you have to start somewhere. Pick the idea that is most appealing to you if you haven't already fixed on a business of your own. As you work through the rest of this and the following steps, your idea will take a much stronger shape.

In the next Personal Workshop you are asked to visualize yourself actually running the business of your dreams. This is an effective way to start to answer "What business are you in?"—and to ensure that the business does indeed accord with your personal goals and values.

Use what you have learned thus far in this guide to help you visualize your business in detail.

Key Note

Wayne Huizenga, present owner of Blockbuster Video, made his first immense fortune by taking over trash management for many municipalities—that is, privatizing what had been a public service.

Personal Workshop # 9
Visualizing My Business

As you visualize your business, think about the following questions:

- How much money are you earning? Be specific: "I'm earning $75, 000 a year" is more powerful than "Lots!"

- What kind of lifestyle are you and your family leading? Visualize in detail.

- How big is your business? (Dollar sales, outlets, employees, or other measures)

- How does your business reflect you and your values?

- What products and services are you offering?

- Imagine your customers. Who are they? How many? What are they like?

- Where is your business located?

- What does your place of business look like?

- Picture your employees. How many do you have? What are they doing? How are you treating them?

- What are you doing in the business? Do you like it?

The Concept: What Business Will You Be In?

This is a tough question. The simple answers, such as "the hardware business" or "I'm in computers" are too simple. They don't give the level of detail that you need for a feasibility analysis.

Now tighten up your business description. You know what business you plan to enter. You have pictured yourself running that business and have thought about its products, services, markets, and general appearance.

Answers to these Five Key Questions will help you refine your business description:

1. *What kind of business are you going to be in?*
   There are four broad categories: Retail, Wholesale, Service, and Manufacturing.

2. *What industry will you be in?*
   Examples would be the hospitality industry (a service sub-category), the publishing industry, the children's clothing industry, or wine industry.

3. *What are your products or services going to be? What are you planning to sell?*
   What products or services do you plan to sell? Be fairly general: "self-help books" or "wine & cheese" or "personal computer training." Don't try to break this down much further at this time.
   Selling specific products or services to specific markets is the heart of your business idea.

4. *Who will your customers be? What are your markets?*
   This is the most important question of all. You have to be able to identify those persons who are most likely to buy your products or services. Know as much as you can reasonably find out about them. Prove that there are enough of those people available to you to make your business work.

5. *What will be special or distinctive about your business? Why will people buy from you rather than from someone else?*
   You need to have something that will set your business apart from your competitors. There are plenty of ways to make your business stand out. The way you choose to make your business different will be a major factor in your success.
   What will be different about your business? You might provide greater convenience, or special expertise in a narrow field, or a better location, or more responsive staff. "Me-too" businesses without any distinctive edge have a rough time surviving.

Personal Workshop Preparation #10: Five Key Questions

Answer the Five Key Questions in the next Personal Workshop and you'll have an answer to "What business will you be in?" Don't worry if it looks like you are in more than one business or industry or have a scattered line of products. Note how our case study entrepreneur, Constance Fisk, completed Personal Workshop #10.

THE PURPOSE OF THIS WORKSHOP IS TO HELP YOU REFINE YOUR BUSINESS DESCRIPTION.

Personal Workshop #10
Five Key Questions

1. What kind of **business** are you going to be in?	custom wedding dress making, a service and specialty manufacturing kind of business
2. What **industry** will you be in?	wedding
3. What are your **products or services** going to be?	custom-designed, handmade wedding gowns and bridesmaid dresses
4. Who will your **customers** be?	brides-to-be within my local market area and county limits, (more or less) and their attendants
5. What will be **special or distinctive** about your business?	My dresses and gowns aren't off-the-rack items but will be unique and priced high. All the other bridal shops in the area compete on price and offer ready-to-wear gowns they "customize."

Note that Constance has defined her market area (local), her target market (local brides and their attendants), her product niche (customized and handmade wedding gowns and dresses), and has even begun a high-price for high-value strategy. This provides a clear description of what her business will be and why it will succeed.

This description will be used to research the market (Step 3 of this guide). Look at #2: "What industry?" The wedding industry is vast—and has a literature all its own, ranging from *Today's Bride* and *Bride* to trade association publications covering every facet of putting on a wedding.

THE PURPOSE OF THIS WORKSHOP IS TO HELP YOU REFINE YOUR BUSINESS DESCRIPTION.

Personal Workshop #10
Five Key Questions

1. What kind of **business** are you going to be in?	
2. What **industry** will you be in?	
3. What are your **products or services** going to be?	
4. Who will your **customers** be?	
5. What will be **special or distinctive** about your business?	

What Will Be Your Competitive Edge?

What will set you apart from your competitors?
Differentiation (or positioning) is arguably the most important small business marketing strategy. Your aim is to locate a **market niche**, a market large enough to be profitable, small enough to defend against other businesses, and suited to your resources, interests, and abilities.

Key Word

Decide ahead of time how you wish to position your business so that you can influence your markets' perceptions of your business. If you plan to sell on quality, you will go one way. If you decide to differentiate your business on grounds of convenience, or price, or durability, you have other options. You cannot follow all of them without hopelessly blurring your image.

> Nordstrom's slogan: *"The only difference between stores is the way they treat customers."*
>
> Marshall Field: *"Give the lady what she wants."*

Here are some ways businesses differentiate their products and services:

- Quality
- Service (courtesy)
- Perceived value
- Convenience
- Reliability
- Price
- Familiarity
- Owned by long-time local resident
- Warranty
- Financing options
- Product range
- Specialization
- Credentials
- Method of production
- Accessibility of purchase
- Prestige
- Status

As you get more familiar with your product or service, markets, and **competition**, you will begin to see other ways to differentiate your business. The image your business projects when it starts will be very hard to change later, if it can be changed at all.

Key Word

When you have completed the preceding Personal Workshop #10: Five Key Questions, and your business idea is taking shape, you have already begun to find a niche for your business. Now you can do some rudimentary competitive research to develop a competitive edge.

- Look for a business that is similar to the one you propose, one that sells the same products or services to the same kinds of markets that you have chosen. The closer the match, the more useful this exercise will be.

Constance Fisk went to several nearby towns where she would not be in direct competition with bridal ships and found a custom wedding gown business that was pretty much like what she had in mind.

- "Shop" that business as if you were their customer. Ask yourself what you like (and dislike) about their:
  - product or service
  - courtesy
  - quality
  - location and appearance of their place of business
  - prices

 Constance Fisk found that while she liked the product, service, and quality of the business, the location was unattractive (in a low-rent district) and the prices were lower than she felt she would charge. Selling expensive, customized wedding gowns cries out for a suitable location and ambiance. You don't sell diamonds at the five-and-dime.

- Look for the points you can improve upon. These will help you differentiate your business from the competition.

 Constance will differentiate her wedding gown business from the bridal shops by (1) focusing on a customized product line, (2) personalizing to a high degree, and (3) locating in a higher rent space than she had originally planned.

Personal Workshop Preparation #11: Going Shopping

Assumption: you have completed the preceding Personal Workshop #10, have a business idea that is taking shape, and have already begun to find a niche for your business—now you can do some rudimentary competitive research to develop a competitive edge. Use Personal Workshop #11 to help you with this process.

Personal Notes

_____

_____

_____

THE PURPOSE OF THIS WORKSHOP IS TO DETERMINE WHAT YOUR COMPETITIVE EDGE WILL BE

Personal Workshop #11
Going Shopping

Look for a business that is similar to the one you propose, one that sells the same products or services to the same kind of markets that you have chosen. The closer the match, the more useful this exercise will be.

List that business here:_____

Now "shop" the business as if you were their customer. Ask yourself what you like (and dislike) about the following areas:

	I Like:	I Dislike:
• product or service		
• courtesy		
• quality		
• location and appearance		
• prices		

If you were to take over this business, what would you do to make it better?

What areas need improving?

Now that you have had an opportunity to "shop" at a similar business, how will your business stand up to the competition? What is *your* competitive edge?

Hold These Questions!

At this point you may have some burning questions such as the following. These are important questions, but they are premature. You can't answer them until you know what your business will be, where it will be located, and how complex your business will be. Some require professional advice from a lawyer or accountant—and at this stage you have neither.

Question 1: *Where can I obtain financing?*
It depends on your business, your location, your resources and your experience.

Question 2: *Should I incorporate my business?*
It depends on the nature of your proposed business, your location, and tax situation.

Question 3: *What permits and licenses do I need?*
It depends on what business you are in, where the business is located, and what you plan to do.

Question 4: *What type of accounting system do I need?*
It depends on the size and nature of your business, your abilities, and your budget.

Question 5: *How do I reserve my business name?*
It depends on the nature of your business and its anticipated markets.

Question 6: *Where can I find a list of venture capitalists?*
At the library, but don't waste your time or theirs. Venture capitalists aren't interested in start-ups unless those start-ups are managed by a highly skilled team with plenty of experience, promise an extraordinarily high rate of return on their investment, and have a definite date when they can get their cash out and reap their reward.

Question 7: *How do I conduct a market survey?*
Carefully.

Key Note

Learn about other businesses by practicing good "networking" skills. See Networking Tips located in the Appendix of this guide.

Good Business Idea or Bad Idea?

A legitimate business idea will stand up to scrutiny. Some ideas do not. They may seem good at first, but when you begin to analyze and research their potential they dissolve into a mishmash of confused markets and products. If your idea is a good one, your market and product focus will become clearer the more you think about it.

Personal Workshop Preparation #12: Weeding the Garden

Ask yourself the following questions about your idea *as it now stands.* A good idea will generate many "YES" responses. A few "NO" responses may indicate that your idea needs some revision before you go on to Step 3, or that you may need more experience (or to find a way to cover the experience gaps), or that you may have cause to drop the idea altogether. A good idea—for you—is one that you approach with enthusiasm and excitement.

As a general rule: Good business ideas are very simple, and become simpler, while bogus ideas generate complexity and confusion as you delve into them.

Personal Notes

_____

_____

_____

Personal Workshop #12
Weeding the Garden

A good business idea will stand out from a bad one as you "weed your garden." Circle yes or no in response to the questions below.

Does your business idea excite you?	Y	N
Can you see yourself running this business—and still smiling?	Y	N
Do you have experience in this kind of business?	Y	N
Do you have management experience?	Y	N
Do you have sales experience?	Y	N
Do you have experience in a related line of business?	Y	N
Do you have other experiences that might help in this business?	Y	N
Is the product or service well-defined and well-focused?	Y	N
Is there an apparent market demand for your products or service?	Y	N
Do you know how to reach that market?	Y	N
Will you have a competitive edge when you are in the market?	Y	N

Is the idea:

• simple?	Y	N
• personalized?	Y	N
• customized or specialized?	Y	N
Do you think you can afford to start such a business?	Y	N

You Have Completed Step 2

If you responded "yes" to the majority of the questions in Personal Workshop #12, you are ready for Step 3: Market Analysis. Your idea may be excellent, and fit well with your values and inclinations, but the key to the success of any business is its ability to secure and retain customers. That will be the next hurdle you will have to leap: Does the idea make good marketing sense?

In this step you learned where most business ideas come from, and have come up with several business ideas you want to pursue. You chose and refined the business idea that most appeals to you, looking at the industry, product or service, markets and competitive edge you could enjoy if you were to start the business. You then visualized that business.

You also have begun to define your product or service and market niche, and have begun to limit your market to those prospects most available to you (a process that will continue in Step 3).

You tested your business idea against the criteria in Personal Workshop #12, and came up with mostly YES responses to the questions in that Workshop.

You Now Will Go Forward to Step 3 with the Following

 Information about sources for business ideas.

 Personal workshops are the tools which can help you evaluate your idea.

 An understanding of how to develop a business idea.

Use this checklist to monitor your progress thus far in this guide. Check off those things you have completed. You may want to go back and complete any activities that you missed.

Step 2
Personal Checklist

❏ Understand where business ideas come from and have begun to make up my own list of possibilities (Personal Workshops #8 and 9).

❏ Answered the 5 Key Questions pertaining to my own business idea (Personal Workshop #10).

❏ Shopped similar businesses to determine what my competition is doing (Personal Workshop #11).

❏ Determined what will make my business successful (Personal Workshop #12).

Step 3

Analyze Your Markets

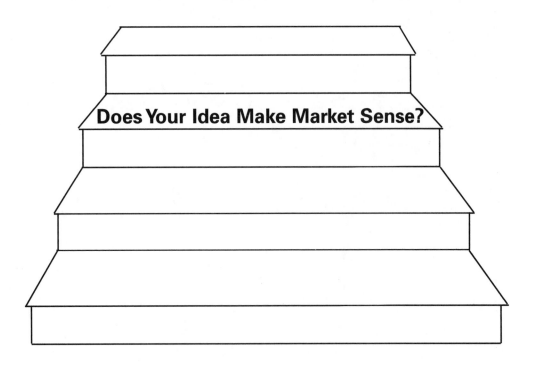

Does Your Idea Make Market Sense?

Step 3

Does Your Idea Make Market Sense?

Sometimes growth comes from unanticipated markets. Oshkosh B'Gosh made bib overalls for farmers and factory workers until 1962, when they placed children's bib overalls in a Miles Kimball mail order catalog as a novelty item. Now 96% of their $365,000,000 annual sales are from children's clothes.

Every aspect of your business revolves around your customers' wants and needs. You have to know what they want, at what price, in what shape or sizes or flavors. You choose your goods and services with your prospective customers in mind. What can you offer your markets that they are ready and eager to buy?

When you complete Step 3, you will be able to:

- Identify trends in your industry and what effect those trends might have on your business idea

- Find out who your customers are (segmentation) and what they want from you (research)

- Analyze your target markets in terms of their geographic, demographic, and psychographic characteristics

- Estimate the size of your markets and your potential market share

- Identify and analyze your competition

- Rethink your competitive edge in light of your analysis of the competition

- Determine whether or not your business makes good marketing sense

Why Market Analysis is Important

Market analysis is a process and a way of thinking about your business. It's a process in which you proceed systematically, answer a series of questions

79

about your markets, and base your answers on facts. It's a way of thinking in which you put your customers' demands at the very center of your business decision-making.

If you don't have a good grasp on who your customers are, you can't effectively advertise your products and services to them. You won't know what messages would appeal to them, where they would see or hear your ads. You choose a location, set working hours, hire and train employees for one purpose: to attract and keep customers.

What's Included in Market Analysis

- What business are you in?

- Who will your customers be?

- Who are your competitors?

To test your business idea or concept, you have to identify and describe your potential customers. You can't know too much about your customers—and you can't afford to guess who they are and what they want.

- Start with industry analysis. What are the trends in your chosen industry? What products, services, and markets are going to be hot?

- Second, perform a market analysis. Who will your customers be? What will they be like? What will they want from you?

- Third, analyze your competition. Is the market big enough to easily accept another competitor (you) or will you have a struggle? How will your business gain and keep a competitive edge?

These three analyses will put your decision about going into business on a firm foundation. Simply hoping the conditions are favorable will not.

Doing a Market Analysis

You need to be creative, persistent, and dig deep when doing your market analysis. Getting detailed information is not easy. There is no substitute for research to test your hunches, make sure that you are moving in the right direction, and be constantly aware that you operate in a competitive market.

 Market analysis saved Ellen Redfern from making a serious mistake. After she abandoned the idea of a computer training business, she investigated another interest: a "green business" which would retail environmentally-friendly products. She found that she was not the first person to light on this idea—

the competition was intense, and none of the stores she walked through were doing well. The market simply was not big enough to permit another entrant.

Being a smart person, she gave up on this business idea, and decided that, for the time being, she would go to work for someone else until she could come up with an idea that made better sense for her.

This is an excellent result. If she had gone ahead without doing her research, she would have put all of her savings at risk and would most likely have failed. Research is a great antidote to entrepreneurial exuberance. Test your idea before committing yourself (e.g., Look before you leap).

Get Help with Your Market Analysis

Don't be afraid to ask for help. Collect as much information as you can yourself for your industry, market and competitor analysis, but don't worry too much about the analysis itself . . . yet. Go see your other resources, those list-

Key Note

> ### The Traditional Approach to Marketing
>
> The 4 P's—Product, Price, Place, and Promotion—are a useful way to remember the traditional elements of marketing. You have to know your *product* (which in this case means "product or service") inside and out—both from your position and, more significantly, from that of your customers, actual or prospective. Next, you need to determine the *price* of your product or service. You have to work within a range of what the market will bear (at one end) and what you can afford to sell the product or service for without losing money at the other end.
>
> *Place* refers to the distribution of the product or service—that is, how the product gets from you to the customer. The location of your business is one of the most critical decisions you will ever make. A manufacturer, for example, has to know how the product will move from the plant to the market—perhaps through a wholesaler or distributor, sometimes through a factory store or other channel. An attorney, on the other hand, might "distribute" legal services in her office, in your office, over the phone, in court, or by mail. Clearly, place, as it pertains to the marketing of certain products and services, can mean more than a geographical location.
>
> The fourth P—*promotion*—encompasses all of the ways you make your goods or services known to your markets. Advertising, public relations, signage, location, and activity in community affairs are just a few of the ways to promote your business.

ed in Step 1, for help with analysis. Research is a learned skill which relies, in part, on using other people's talents. Librarians and other professionals know how and where to dig for information. They can streamline and simplify your research. Get the information first. Then get help interpreting it.

Industry Analysis: What's Happening in Your Industry?

What is industry analysis—and why is it important? Industry analysis helps you answer questions such as:

- What's going on in your industry? Is it growing, stagnating, or shrinking?

- What are the trends in your industry?

- Are these trends national? Do they apply locally?

- Who are the customers for other businesses in your industry?

- What makes those people and people like them buy products or services similar to yours? What are they willing to pay? How far will they go and what will they put up with in order to buy?

All things being equal, you will do better to enter a growing industry rather than one in decline. It's easier to succeed in a growing field than in a shrinking one.

What Industry Are You In?

Your business will be a small part of a large industry. A bookstore is part of the *retailing industry*, although it is only one of many specific types of retailing. A publisher (whether large-print or not) is in the *printing and publishing industry,* which is part of the manufacturing sector. A bed-and-breakfast business is part of the *hospitality industry*, which in turn is part of the service sector of the economy. A dentist is in the *health care industry*, which is part of the service sector.

You may be in more than one industry. As an example, a computer consultant may be part of the *computer industry*, or she may be part of the *business services industry*, or both! A computer retailer may be in the *retailing industry*, but if he also repairs computer equipment, he will be in the *business services industry.*

So what industry are you in? There are several ways to find out.

- If you are going to be in retail, your industry usually will be defined by the products or product lines you sell. If you want to start a hardware store, you would probably classify yourself as being in the hardware industry. However, depending on the specific product lines you carry in your store, you might consider yourself to be in the tool industry or the building materials industry.

- If you are planning a service business, what service are you planning to provide? Accountants are in the accounting services industry. Doctors are in the health services industry. Beauticians may be in the beauty industry, or they may think of themselves as being in the hairdressing industry or the cosmetology industry.

- What trade association(s) will you be joining? What trade publications will you subscribe to? What trade shows will you attend? The answers to these questions will help you define your industry.

- If you still cannot find the appropriate industry for your proposed business, go to the library and look in the index of the Standard Industrial Classification Manual. The SIC Manual can usually be found in the reference section of the library. Still stumped? Ask the librarian for help.

Constance Fisk found two classifications in the SIC Manual that included bridal gowns:

SIC 2335: Woman's, misses', and juniors' dresses (manufacturing), and

SIC 5621: Women's clothing stores (retail).

Upon closer examination, however, Constance discovered that her business really fit into SIC 2335 and not SIC 5621. She makes custom wedding gowns, which is a form of manufacturing. Although she also sells the gowns she makes directly to her customers, SIC 5621 does not include bridal shops that sell custom made wedding gowns. Constance never thought of herself as a manufacturer, but she really is!

Dennis Aney's business is SIC 3672 (printed circuit boards manufacturing). The two-digit code "36" represents the Major Group "Electronic and Electrical Equipment Manufacturing"; the three-digit code "367" identifies the Industry Group "Electric Components and Accessories"; and the four-digit code "3672" identifies his Specific Industry Group.

Once he knew his SIC code, Dennis was able to locate more information about his industry:

- Using the Census of Manufacturers he found out how many direct competitors he had in his state, the average number of employees per firm, and total annual sales volume for all firms in SIC 3672.

- Using his state's directory of manufacturers he found out who his direct competitors were and where they were located.

- Using the U.S. Industrial Outlook he found one- and five-year forecasts for his industry, including statistics for expected sales growth industry-wide.

Table 3.1 is a list of the SIC codes and descriptions for the start-up entrepreneurs you are following in this guide.

Table 3.1: Smart Steps Start-up Entrepreneurs and Their SIC Codes

Entrepreneur	SIC Code	Description
Constance Fisk	2335	Women's, misses', and juniors' dresses
Ellen Redfern	8243	Data processing schools
Dave Campbell	5921	Liquor stores
	5451	Dairy products stores
Dennis Aney	3672	Printed circuit boards
Phillip Treleven	2731	Books: publishing and printing
The Sandlers	7011	Hotels and motels

What Are the Trends and Outlook for Your Industry?

All industries go through a life cycle which has four broad cycles: embryo, growth, maturity, and decline.

Key Note

SIC Codes

Standard Industrial Classification (SIC) codes are especially useful for industry analysis. Once you know the SIC for your industry you can conduct secondary research using readily available sources to gather statistics, trend data, and other information about your industry. Later in this guide you will see how segmentation of markets on the basis of SIC is also effective for industrial or business-to-business firms.

Figure 3.1: Life Cycle of an Industry

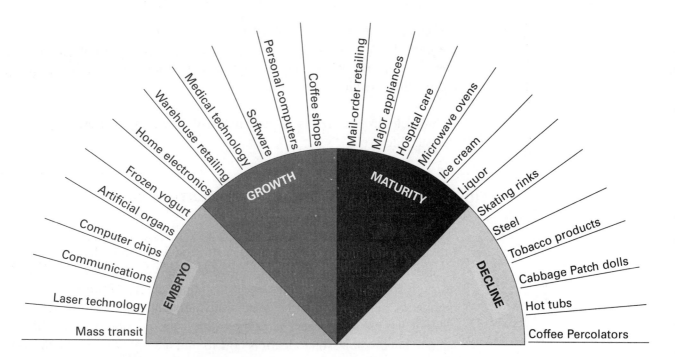

Each stage of the life cycle can present excellent business opportunities—and each stage presents its own set of dangers.

As an example, when VCRs were beginning to gain popularity, thousands of entrepreneurs hopped on the VCR bandwagon and opened video rental stores. This is characteristic of the *embryonic* stage: low cost of entry, a chaotic market, scattered competition, and a growing consumer demand. The video store industry then entered a *growth* phase, characterized by explosive growth in the number of stores, considerably more sophisticated competition, and a more demanding market. A lot of the early video stores failed in this period due to lack of capital and lack of a coherent marketing plan.

It is now entering its *mature* phase: it is much more stable, it is beginning to consolidate (look at the growth by acquisition of Blockbuster Video and other chains), and the cost of entry is high due to inventory needs (more titles, more copies of hot titles), location, delivery costs, and fierce price competition.

The next phase, *decline*, isn't far off due to new technologies such as satellite delivery. Cable and telephone companies are going to offer movies-on-demand. Kiosks in grocery stores and shopping malls are already competing on price for the home market. Decline is marked by sharply lower profitability, increased price competition, and a trend towards fewer but larger players.

You can make money in any of these phases. Embryonic and growth stages are more hospitable to the small operator than maturity or decline—but there will always be exceptions. And some industries are much slower to change than the video rental industry.

In broad terms, the trends in your industry are set by its position on the industry life cycle.

How and Where to Find Information

Take Your Librarian to Lunch

Librarians are the most underutilized professionals around. They are trained as researchers and will (usually) be glad to help you design and pursue a research study. Their resources are astounding, ranging from the obvious (books) to the mysterious (the "electronic highway" and the obscure pathways of the Internet). These resources vary from one library to another—but one important lesson to learn is how to find the right expert to help you solve problems. And market research *is* a problem. There is so much information out there that without a structured approach you can waste years wandering the information corridors with no results. What this means is that you must sift, skim, and analyze. Remember, the process of finding information is an ongoing one.

Personal Experience

Personal experience will guide your research efforts. You know a great deal—more than you may realize—about your industry from general reading and observation. Your interest in the specific business you are now evaluating is based, at least to some degree, on your insights into how the business operates and how the industry it is in is faring. Don't ignore these insights. Check them out (that's what research is for) but do not ignore them.

Business Periodicals

Business periodicals are a good source of general industry trend information. National magazines (such as *Business Week*, *Forbes*, and *Fortune*) run articles describing industry trends, especially if they indicate some major change in the way the industry operates. Local business magazines and newspapers also cover trends, usually from a local slant. These are broad-brush approaches, so the next step is to find out what's going on in greater detail. Trade associations exist to fill this need.

Trade Associations

Trade associations are an excellent source of specific business and industry trends. You aren't the only person interested in getting accurate market information. Trade associations offer their members information as the primary reason to join up and pay dues. Trade association spin-offs—trade magazines, trade shows, and exhibitions—afford chances to learn what other, similar businesses are up to. And with over 35,000 trade associations listed in the *Encyclopedia of Associations* (Gale Research, Detroit, MI) in the United States alone, chances are excellent that you can glean some very useful market information.

Trade Data

Trade data is found in trade publications, the magazines and articles put out by trade associations. You will find trade publications listed in the *Encyclopedia of Associations* and the *Small Business Sourcebook*. Check your library for other reference books covering periodicals. The *Encyclopedia of Business Information Sources*, another Gale Research product, covers general works, directories, ratios, handbooks and manuals, periodicals and newsletters, on-line databases, statistics sources, and more.

Trade data is especially helpful for locating answers to questions that other business owners and their advisors have had. What are the trends? What market techniques are effective? Who are the most likely purchasers—and what are their demographics? What pricing strategies work? Who is entering or leaving the industry?

Make sure that the information you get is really appropriate for your particular business. Generalized trade data is tricky to apply to a fledgling venture in the here and now.

Government Publications

Government publications are worth looking at. The Small Business Administration (SBA) has an extensive list of free or low-cost publications, some of which are aimed at specific industries, some at specific businesses. They maintain two helpful telephone lines: the SBA Hot Line (900-463-4636) and SBA Technical Support line (202-265-6400).

Private Research Firms

Research companies will dig up industry and market information for you, but they are not inexpensive. They are fast, expert, and discreet, so if your business is going to call for a substantial investment you might want to enlist their help. Locate private research firms in the telephone book.

On-Line Sources

CompuServe and America Online are two of the on-line services that provide inexpensive access to a wide range of information resources. (These require monthly fees.) Some of these will cost extra: specialized databases like NEXIS, services such as Dow-Jones News Retrieval, or highly specialized newsletters which cover a specific industry aren't free.

Both AOL and CompuServe offer many small business "chat groups" and resource centers. The chat groups offer help and advice for people entering, for example, computer graphics-based businesses, retailers of all kinds, most professional services, and even more. This is a growing source of information well worth checking out. Microsoft subsidizes a small business resource center which offers advice on everything from starting to selling a small business, computer-related or not. Some small business magazines run forums to discuss trends and ideas and opportunities: *Entrepreneur,* for example, is on CompuServe.

 Phillip Treleven's experience in the large-print industry made his market research stunningly simple: He knew that the industry trends for large-print books were very positive. Two demographic trends fueled this growth: people are living longer, and the Baby Boomers are reaching middle age. Therefore more and more people will be using large-print books. He surveyed the 22,000 libraries in the U.S. that are the prime market for large-print books and solicited the opinions and desires of the librarians who do the buying by asking them questions such as:

• What do you want for your readers?

• What kinds of books aren't available that should be?

• Would you prefer to order from a catalog, sales person, or by phone?

He was mobbed. Response rates shot up over 80 percent. *Nobody had thought of asking the librarians what they wanted for their readers!* It turned out that large-print readers are like other readers. They wanted to have best sellers, mysteries, romances, history books, and so on. He followed their advice and signed up Penguin Books and Harlequin Romances, struck deals with general publishers for large-print reprint rights, and revolutionized the large-print market.

Key Note

Be careful! You can do too much research. Watch out—it's addictive.

Furthermore, *nobody had thought of asking librarians how they preferred to buy large-print books.* Most wanted a program with negative option: send package A, B, or C unless informed otherwise. If he cared enough to solic-it and trust their judgment, they would trust his. Talk about a competitive advantage!

Personal Workshop Preparation #13: Identify Your Industry Trends

In Personal Workshop #13, you will have to do some library research to determine your industry classification, trade associations, and key trade publications. You can use these sources to identify the important trends in your industry.

Personal Notes

_____

_____

_____

Key Note

The Desktop Business Intelligence Sourcebook: A Comprehensive Guidebook for the Information Age (Hyde Park Marketing Group: Cincinnati, OH, 1992) is a useful entry point to the rapidly expanding num-ber of electronic information sources. On-line resources are valuable assets to you in your marketing research and analysis. Don't overlook them.

Personal Workshop #13
Identify Your Industry Trends

Determine your SIC code. Look in the *Standard Industrial Classification Code Manual's* index to identify your business's 4-digit SIC code.

My **SIC** Code is: 2335

Consult other reference books such as the *Encyclopedia of Associations* or *The Small Business Sourcebook*. These will steer you to the major trade associations and the major trade publications for your business.

My **national** trade association is: National Bridal Service

    Their address and telephone number are:

    3122 W. Cary Street

    Richmond, VA 23221

    804-355-6945

My **regional** or local trade association is:

    Their address and telephone number are:

The most important **trade publications** for my industry are:

1. *Bridal Trends*

2. *Elegant Brides*

3. *Modern Bride*

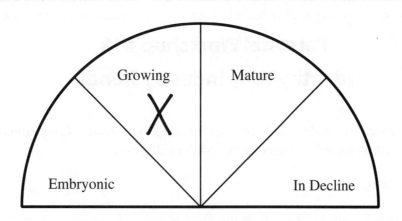

Industry Life Cycle

According to my trade association and trade publications, the major trends in my industry are:

a. Place an X on the Life Cycle where your industry is today. Is it embryonic, growing, mature, or in decline?

b. The **hot products** in this industry are:

Custom wedding dresses, veils, and <u>accessories.</u>

c. The **hot markets** for this industry are:

Formal/traditional, but very specialized weddings.
Wedding services are in!

d. Declining products and markets for this industry are:

Rubber stamp weddings - out!
Custom, specialized weddings - in!

Personal Workshop #13
Identify Your Industry Trends

Determine your SIC code. Look in the *Standard Industrial Classification Code Manual's* index to identify your business's 4-digit SIC code.

My **SIC** Code is:

Consult other reference books such as the *Encyclopedia of Associations* or *The Small Business Sourcebook*. These will steer you to the major trade associations and the major trade publications for your business.

My **national** trade association is:

    Their address and telephone number are:

My **regional** or local trade association is:

    Their address and telephone number are:

The most important **trade publications** for my industry are:

1.

2.

3.

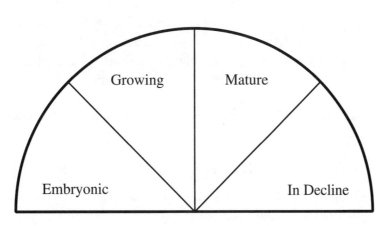

Industry Life Cycle

According to my trade association and trade publications, the major trends in my industry are:

a.   Place an X on the Life Cycle where your industry is today. Is it embryonic, growing, mature, or in decline?

b.   The **hot products** in this industry are:

c.   The **hot markets** for this industry are:

d.   Declining products and markets for this industry are:

What Are You Selling?

Customers don't buy products or services. They buy benefits, the "what's in it for me?" that spurs them to buy. The benefits they perceive are often not those that you have spotted, which is why surveys and other methods to find out what your customers want are so important.

You have to look at your offerings from your customers' points of view.

- How do they perceive your products or services?

- Why would they buy from you—and not from others?

- What can you do to make it easier, more fun, more convenient, safer for them to buy from you?

- What are your competitors doing to woo customers—and can you find out what your customers are looking for? What works for them and what does not?

People won't buy goods and services they don't want, no matter how powerful the advertising and positioning. You can only sell them what they want to buy. Sometimes that will be what they need. But it will seldom be what you think you are selling.

 Dave Campbell began his market research by looking in his area for other wine stores. He found that there was but one specialty wine retailer in his MSA (Metropolitan Statistical Area), and knew from trade publications that, for stores such as his, a base population of 140,000 would easily support another specialty wine store.

His competition would include liquor stores, supermarkets, and a few major discounters. He defined his niche, marketing primarily to upper income retirees, "yuppies," and professional/managerial. He would be selling an education in wine as much as the wine itself, along with some wine snobbery and status. By focusing on this niche, he could stand out from and avoid much of the impact of the price choppers. While he couldn't afford to sell Beaujolais Nouveau at two percent over cost in case lots the way the discount store could, he wouldn't have to.

Personal Workshop Preparation #14:
Features and Benefits of My Product or Service

In the next Personal Workshop, start looking at *your* products or service from two points of view. The first is "What are the features of my products or service?" The second is "What are the benefits of my products or service?"

As a preview of Personal Workshop #14, Dave Campbell approached the features and benefits of his base products in this way:

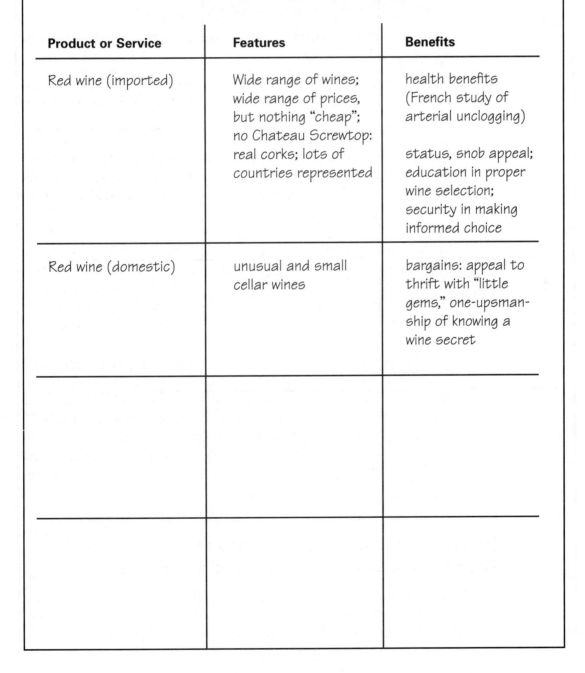

THE PURPOSE OF THIS WORKSHOP IS TO IDENTIFY THE FEATURES AND BENEFITS OF YOUR PRODUCT OR SERVICE.

Personal Workshop #14

Features and Benefits
of My Product or Service

Product or Service	Features	Benefits
Red wine (imported)	Wide range of wines; wide range of prices, but nothing "cheap"; no Chateau Screwtop: real corks; lots of countries represented	health benefits (French study of arterial unclogging) status, snob appeal; education in proper wine selection; security in making informed choice
Red wine (domestic)	unusual and small cellar wines	bargains: appeal to thrift with "little gems," one-upsmanship of knowing a wine secret

THE PURPOSE OF THIS WORKSHOP IS TO IDENTIFY THE FEATURES AND BENEFITS OF YOUR PRODUCT OR SERVICE.

Personal Workshop #14

Features and Benefits
of My Product or Service

Product or Service	Features	Benefits
1.		
2.		
3.		
4.		

Market Analysis: Finding Customers

Eighty percent of your profits will come from 20 percent of your customers. Who will that 20 percent be? Where can you find those customers? Your answers come from market analysis.

Market analysis helps you answer questions such as:

- What markets should you approach with your products and services?

- Who are your target markets, those groups of persons most likely to buy from you?

- What is your market niche?

- What is your market area?

- How big is your market?

- What are the characteristics of your markets?

Suppose Constance Fisk had discovered that there were dozens of competitors in her town, none of whom made a living because the competition was so intense.

Constance Fisk, the wedding dress maker, did the obvious things first. How could she find out how many brides per year would be likely customers for wedding dresses in her market area? As you will see, this took some digging.

Limit the scope of your research and analysis. Narrow the funnel. You start with that large group of people or businesses who *might* buy your product or service, then narrow that group down to a target market which consists of those people *most likely* to be your customers.

Who Will Buy Your Product(s) or Service?

Don't assume that your market consists of everyone. It doesn't. At best you will have only a percentage of your market (your "market share"), because some people in your markets will move, leave the market, go to competitors, spend their money on something else, or won't know you exist. You can only serve a limited geographical area (with a few exceptions such as mail order). People don't go huge distances to buy a product or service without a compelling reason.

Culling your market to that core target market makes it possible for you to spend your promotional money wisely, get to know your customers in depth, and to keep a balance between the size of your business and the size of your market.

Define the Markets You Will Be Serving

There are several ways to define and limit your markets.

- You can initially limit your markets *geographically*: You will draw customers from within a limited geographic area.

Key Word

- You can limit it further with **demographics**: If you will be selling to consumers, the age, sex, income level, occupation, or educational level of the people in your market are often used to specify who the market really is.

- If you will be selling to other businesses or organizations, you will be interested in demographics such as Standard Industrial Classification (SIC) code, number of employees, number of production workers, annual sales volume, and number of establishments to define and limit your markets.

Key Word

- You can limit it even further using **psychographics**: This refers to the lifestyles of your target customers. What are their attitudes, opinions, and interests? Psychographics will not be very useful if you are planning to sell to other businesses.

- You can also limit your markets in terms of buying situations: Are your customers light, medium, or heavy users of your product? How much effort do they put into shopping for your product or the kind of store at which they prefer to shop? Are they first-time buyers or is this something they buy regularly?

Sources of Information

Dealing directly, face-to-face with your market, is called primary research. You gain a lot of information about your proposed market by simply talking with people who use or might use your products or service.

How can you find out why people will buy from you? Ask them. Give them a structure. A questionnaire can be designed to elicit information about who your customers and prospects will be, their buying habits, their opinions of your product or service, and their favored media.

You can ask non-competitive competitors: business owners who are not in your market area. If you call them ahead of time to set a date, send them a short list of questions you want to get answers to, and set a time limit to your visit, you will more often than not get a positive response and a ton of good information. The key is the list of questions and the businesslike approach.

Secondary research is less personal. It serves two important purposes. First, it can show you the kinds of questions and results other business owners and other experts have worked with in the past, thus widening your horizons and giving you inexpensive information. This can save time as well if you don't have to repeat the surveys or interviews. Second, it can multiply your experience at no cost, save a few hours of your time.

Define Your Target Market

Ask yourself: "Who needs my goods and services?" Start with those people you feel will most likely be your customers. If you plan to sell theatrical makeup, asking this question would yield such answers as actors, directors, theater organizations, and other kinds of performers—and perhaps trick-or-treaters. Who are the people with the most obvious need for your product or service—and the easiest for you to reach?

All buying decisions are made by individuals, and are ultimately subjective. For this reason alone, your chances of success are enhanced by your familiarity with people in your **target markets**. Few things are less rewarding and more costly than selling into markets you know little or nothing about.

There is an important relationship between the size of your business and the size of your target markets. If you choose markets that are too large for you, you won't be able to afford to promote your business to that market, nor can you gain much presence in the market. The classic example of trying to gain entry into too wide a market is the new venture owner who crows, "If we only get one-eighth of a percent of this $1.6 billion market, we'll have sales of $2 million a year!" Not only is this a turn-off for any investor or banker, it also leads to disastrous business decisions. Since your resources are limited, limit your markets. You want to at least be able to make your better prospects aware of who you are and what you can do for them.

"Segmentation is the process of identifying groups of customers with enough characteristics in common to make possible the design and presentation of a product or service each group needs."

—James L. Heskett,
Harvard Business School,
quoted in *Davidson & Uttall*, p. 54

Key Word

Market Segmentation

Market segmentation is a method of organizing and categorizing those persons or organizations that you think will buy your products. It amounts to looking at your customers and noting their obvious characteristics, then looking to wider markets for more groups of people with the same (or similar) characteristics. For example, suppose you are selling computerized account-

Key Word

Key Note

If you have no competitors, you either don't have a viable business idea, or you haven't come to grips with what business you are really in. Theodore Levitt, in a classic essay entitled "Marketing Myopia," noted that, some years ago, Hollywood decided it was in the movie business, and television was not competition. After losing billions of dollars of business to this newer medium, Hollywood finally realized it was in the entertainment business, not just movies, and began to compete successfully.

ing services to small business owners and that you have several auto dealers who are delighted with your service and expertise. Build on your strength: you have expertise in the auto dealer market. Look for more auto dealerships in the same size range and in the same geographic area first. Then look for similar businesses (truck dealers, tractor dealers) to widen your market. Or, if you are most successful working with women who own auto dealerships, look for more dealerships (auto, truck, farm equipment, etc.) owned by women. The rule here is that success leads to more success—so once you have good customers, find more people who are similar to those good customers. That's all you are trying to do when you segment your market.

Suppose your business is selling comic books. A demographic survey of your customer base would probably tell you that your typical "hot prospect" is male, in his early 20s, has a low income, and is primarily a student rather than employed (see Table 3.2). Even with only this demographic information, you'd have a valuable (and market-defining) customer profile on which to base further research to make the profile more precise.

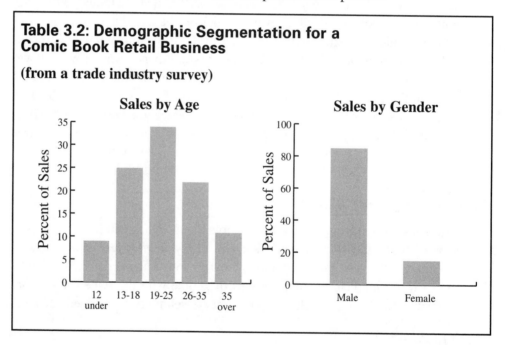

Table 3.2: Demographic Segmentation for a Comic Book Retail Business

(from a trade industry survey)

Estimate the Market Potential

How big is your market? Sometimes this is easy to figure out. If you are selling to a local market, you can get census data and maps which show you how many people live or work within your market area. You can get traffic counts if that is important: often these will be available from local sources such as Chambers of Commerce or banks. Economic planning commissions and departments can help you if you can tell them clearly what your market area is and what kind of people within that area you hope to identify.

If your market is business-to-business, you can get a count of prospective customers from mailing lists (check the Standard Rate & Data Service in your library). Check the Yellow Pages and contact the Chamber of Commerce for information on local businesses. Sometimes you have to be clever and persistent, but ordinarily you can get a rough fix on the size of your market through these kinds of sources.

 Constance Fisk's research showed a strong trend towards formal weddings in her area. Ten years ago a business specializing in custom-made wedding dresses would have been tough to start; informality reigned. Demographic and industry research showed that an increasing percentage of brides are in their late 20s or early 30s, spend their own money on customized wedding dresses, and are much less price-sensitive than a younger population who rely on their parents. (Fathers tend to blanch at the cost of wedding gowns.)

Now her question became this: Will there be enough brides in the 28-35 year old range, in her area, to specialize? Or should she widen her market to include more brides, perhaps segmenting them by income or address?

There is no right answer to these kinds of questions. Constance decided to follow her intuition and aim directly for the 28-35 year old brides. No one else in her geographic market area was target marketing more specifically than "young women" which would provide a positioning hook for her. No one else was designing and sewing customized wedding gowns—or if they could, weren't advertising that they had the capability.

Constance figures that she will have to serve 30 weddings a year at an average of $2,000 per wedding to reach her financial goals. She called her local papers and got a rough figure of the number of formal weddings in her market area for the past year: 12 to 25 per week, depending on the season, or about 750 per year. That meant that she would have to capture four percent of the market, a figure she felt she could reach.

Personal Workshop Preparation #15: Segmenting My Market—Consumer and Industrial

When you segment your market for consumers in Personal Workshop #15, use a broadbrush approach. Are your customers young, middle-aged, old? Are they rich, poor, middle income? Are they high school or college graduates? Do they live in an identifiable neighborhood or local area?

If you are selling to other businesses or organizations instead of consumers, use your SIC code, your geographic location, size characteristics, and other variables such as product use, service requirements, and purchasing policies to segment the market.

THE PURPOSE OF THIS WORKSHOP IS TO DETERMINE WHO YOUR CUSTOMERS WILL BE, IF YOU WILL BE SELLING TO OTHER BUSINESSES OR ORGANIZATIONS INSTEAD OF (OR IN ADDITION TO) CONSUMERS.

Personal Workshop #15
Segmenting My Market-Consumer

Age (range)
28-35 years

**Sex
(Male or Female)**
Female/Male contribute financially

Income (range)
Female $36,000 yr.   Male $40,000 yr.

Occupation
Employed

Educational Level
College education

Home Address
Suburbs

Lifestyle
Couples are <u>very</u> busy.
Little time/want personalized services!

Etc.
Custom work—Unique weddings

Segmenting My Market—Industrial

Standard Industrial Classification (SIC) code (4-digit preferred)

3663 - Broadcasting & Comm. Equip.

3625 - Relays & Ind. Controls

3812 - Navigation Syst. & Instr.

3823 - Industrial Instruments

Geographic location, e.g., counties, metro areas, state, multi-state region, nation, multi-nation region, etc.

Wisconsin, Minnesota, and northern Illinois

Size characteristics, e.g., annual sales volume, purchase volume, number of employees/production workers, number of establishments, etc.

- less than $10 million annual sales

- Usually single plant operations

- Customers usually require less than $100,000 of product (small contracts)

Other variables, e.g., how product is used, buy class, service requirements, purchasing policies, and/or many others

Product is used as component part.

May be new, buy, or rebuy situation

Bidding for blanket contracts for 24-hour delivery

THE PURPOSE OF THIS WORKSHOP IS TO DETERMINE WHO YOUR CUSTOMERS WILL BE, IF YOU WILL BE SELLING TO OTHER BUSINESSES OR ORGANIZATIONS INSTEAD OF (OR IN ADDITION TO) CONSUMERS.

Personal Workshop #15
Segmenting My Market—Consumer

Age (range)	
Sex (Male or Female)	
Income (range)	
Occupation	
Educational Level	
Home Address	
Lifestyle	
Etc.	

Segmenting My Market—Industrial

Standard Industrial Classification (SIC) code (4-digit preferred)

Geographic location, e.g., counties, metro areas, state, multi-state region, nation, multi-nation region, etc.

Size characteristics, e.g., annual sales volume, purchase volume, number of employees/production workers, number of establishments, etc.

Other variables, e.g., how product is used, buy class, service requirements, purchasing policies, and/or many others

Is There Room for You?

Now ask if there is room for another competitor—you—in this market.

During your research into trade information you may have come up with statistics suggesting the number of people required to support the type of business you want to start. This is called the *threshold level*, the minimum market size necessary to support a given type of business.

If your business showed that 10,000 people are needed to support a hardware store, and your market area has 40,000 people, then you might conclude that four hardware stores would fill the market. If there are three stores now, there may be room for another. If there are six stores already, there probably is not enough room for another competitor.

Threshold analysis can be a handy tool, but you should be careful when using it to determine if there is room in the market for you. One large, efficient hardware store may adequately serve the market of 40,000 people. Consider the presence of competitors such as discount building supplies stores. If there are six stores in a market that theoretically can support only four stores, it doesn't automatically mean there's no room for your store. If your store will do a better job of meeting the needs of the market, customers may throng to your store. Use threshold analysis as a preliminary indicator, but always dig deeper and look closer at your market.

Competitor Analysis: Scouting the Competition

What is competitor analysis and why is it important?

Competitive analysis helps you answer questions such as:

- Who are your direct competitors?
- Who are your indirect competitors?
- How and what can you learn from your competition?
- How does your competitive edge hold up?

> *Compete, don't envy.*
> —Arabian Proverb

Every business has competition. You want to learn who they are and what they are doing. If a market is over-served (too many competitors) you might want to change your plans.

Who Will You be Competing Against?

Identifying direct competition is easy.

Look in the yellow pages, the same way most consumers do, and see how many competitors are listed. Walk up and down Main Street if you will be a retailer located on Main Street. Check local newspapers if your market is local; you want to see who is in the market and who is entering or leaving the market. If you have a local newspaper, pay a visit to the business editor. Try to buy the product or service: the way you go about finding a supplier is the same as anyone else does.

If your markets are not local, the problem of identifying your competition is no more complicated. Suppose you sell a product to manufacturers. There are books listing manufacturers. For instance, *Thomas's Register*, found in almost every library, lists manufacturers nationwide. State economic departments maintain lists of manufacturers within the state. These can yield helpful prospect lists as well as help you learn the size of the market. Trade publications that accept ads are a good way to identify competitors: Who is buying ad space? Ask for a *media kit* which will give you information about the size and characteristics of the readership—and give you several issues so you can see who advertises.

Indirect competitors are those who are selling products or services to your markets (while not exactly what you are selling): they compete for your markets' dollar. For example, makers of hand-held electronic games have to contend with growing indirect competition from games on personal computers. With the advent of CD-rom technology, and smaller personal computers, this indirect competition will only increase.

> *Of all human powers operating on the affairs of mankind, none is greater than that of competition.*
>
> —Henry Clay

Personal Workshop Preparation #16: Who Is My Competition?

Find out who your competitors are. Begin your study by naming your competitors in the next Personal Workshop.

Before you begin, observe how Constance Fisk completed Personal Workshop #16. Note who she listed as her competitors.

Personal Notes

_____

_____

Personal Workshop #16
Who Is My Competition?

Make a list of the competitors with whom you would be in direct competition. Then list those who would be considered indirect or potential competitors.

My direct competitors are:

1.   Bridal Party

2.   Designs by Shelly

3.

4.

5.

Other competitors (include indirect and potential competitors):

1. Jackson's Department Store

2. Brides-to-be

3. Freedman's

4.

5.

Personal Workshop #16
Who Is My Competition?

Make a list of the competitors with whom you would be in direct competition. Then list those who would be considered indirect or potential competitors.

My direct competitors are:

1.

2.

3.

4.

5.

Other competitors (include indirect and potential competitors):

1.

2.

3.

4.

5.

Gather Information about Competitors

Now that you have a list of competitors—start to find out about them. All businesses have competition. List your five closest direct competitors and begin to collect information on them. Clip copies of their advertisements, jot down notes on your observations of them, pay them visits as a customer. Put all of this in your 3-ring binder and in a few weeks you will be amazed at how much you learn about your competition.

Questions you may wish to raise are:

What markets are they pursuing and how? Look at their advertisements and other promotions. Speak to their customers. Shop them. Look at who goes into their store or office. Talk with vendor and suppliers.

How big are they? In dollar sales, number of employees, or any other measure. Are they part of a larger business, or are they independent? (If they are part of a bigger business you may be able to get information on them from annual reports.)

How long have they been in business? Longevity can be a powerful competitive tool.

Any fact or figures you can get will help you understand them better. If you limit your research to a few direct competitors, you can get more valuable information, in more depth, than if you try to understand every possible competitor. Keep this simple.

Research can be straightforward. The Sandlers started by counting the number of B&B's in the yellow pages of their phone book. They found 49 potential competitors, and noted that only one ran a two inch ad. They checked out several tour and guide books from their library to see if any local B&B's were listed. Three were. They got an American Automobile Association tour guide for their state and checked out local competitors—and found that there were several who were not listed in the yellow pages.

Trade association information was not encouraging. Their area was over-B&B'ed, with little differentiation among the competitors. The main claims to fame were historical buildings, central location, or great views, and "excellent muffins."

Following advice from some non-local B&B owners they met on their travels, the Sandlers then turned their attention to business meeting planners, wedding consultants, bridal shop owners, caterers, and florists. This turned up a need for a mid-priced meeting place with limited overnight accommodations, a niche that they plan to explore.

Personal Workshop Preparation #17: How Do My Competitors Compete?

For Personal Workshop #17, make several copies of the information gathering form, one for each competitor you wish to learn more about. How are they competing? What are they promoting, advertising, using to set themselves apart? This workshop is best done in the field—visit the competitor, see where and how they advertise, speak with their vendors, customers, and other interested parties.

As a preview of the next Workshop, observe how Constance Fisk completed the form for one of her competitors.

THE PURPOSE OF THIS WORKSHOP IS TO LEARN MORE ABOUT YOUR COMPETITION

Personal Workshop #17
How Do My Competitors Compete?

Competitor: Designs by Shelly

Describe this competitor's:

Price   Quality and price are lower than my product.

Service   Only dresses—no accessories available

Convenience   Is quick to get dress ready!

Location   Out of her home

Advertising   Word-of-mouth

Other ways to compete (specify)

   Advertise! Yellow pages, sign, local newspaper

   Market to 28-35 age group

   High-end, custom designs

THE PURPOSE OF THIS WORKSHOP IS TO LEARN MORE ABOUT YOUR COMPETITION

Personal Workshop #17
How Do My Competitors Compete?

Competitor:

Describe this competitor's:

Price

Service

Convenience

Location

Advertising

Other ways to compete (specify):

Your Competitive Edge

You will partially define your business by your competition. Most businesses operate within fairly tight parameters: All grocery stores carry more or less the same items. One hardware store is very much like another. Lawyers are interchangeable. Within these limits of product, service, and distribution, there are plenty of ways to set yourself apart. A grocery store might offer a particularly wide range of frozen goods. A hardware store might have a strong automobile parts division. A lawyer might specialize in estate plans for small business owners.

Now that you know what your competition is doing, revisit Personal Workshop #11: Going Shopping. How would you now, given what you know, improve or change your competitive edge?

Personal Workshop Preparation #18: What Am I Going to Do About It?

Understanding the competition is an essential part of marketing. Your promotional strategies and sales success will be influenced by your ability to differentiate your business from your competition. If you know what your competitors are up to, you are well started on the path of differentiating your business from theirs.

What will you do to compete? Use the next Personal Workshop to help you come up with ideas that will set you apart from the competition.

Personal Notes

_____

_____

_____

Personal Workshop #18
What Am I Going to Do About It?

Brainstorm to come up with competitive edge ideas. This should be fun to do as well as informative.

Try "The 10-Minute Solo Brainstorming Technique." Here's how it works:

Generate as many ideas as you can in a 10-minute period. Write them down, sketch them, talk into a tape recorder. Your goal is to generate ideas without editing or criticizing them. You want quantity. The more the merrier.

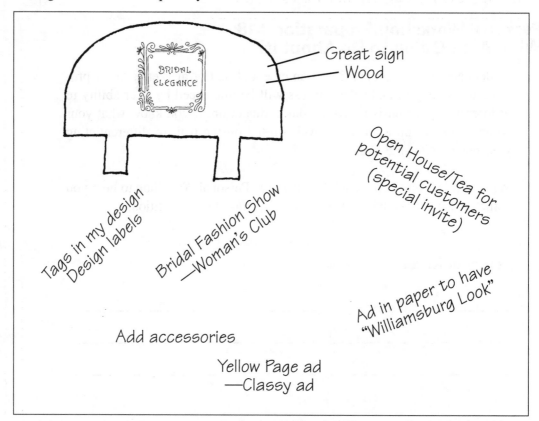

Now take some of your best (or wackiest) ideas and bounce them off your buddies. Which ideas might work? Which ones will you use to compete? Apply the basic brainstorming technique: the more ideas you can come up with, the better the chances that one or more will lead to a strong competitive edge.

THE PURPOSE OF THIS WORKSHOP IS TO HELP YOU RETHINK YOUR COMPETITIVE EDGE

Personal Workshop #18
What Am I Going to Do About It?

Brainstorm to come up with competitive edge ideas. This should be fun to do as well as informative.

Try "The 10-Minute Solo Brainstorming Technique." Here's how it works:

Generate as many ideas as you can in a 10-minute period. Write them down, sketch them, talk into a tape recorder. Your goal is to generate ideas without editing or criticizing them. You want quantity. The more the merrier.

Now take some of your best (or wackiest) ideas and bounce them off your buddies. Which ideas might work? Which ones will you use to compete? Apply the basic brainstorming technique: the more ideas you can come up with, the better the chances that one or more will lead to a strong competitive edge.

Rethinking Your Competitive Edge

You may very well find that you have to rethink what will set you apart. Business owners who are successful enough to stay in business are shrewd enough to have found ways to make their businesses stand out, and you may find that they have already seized "your" competitive edge. That's OK; you can always do something else, or do what they do better, or find a way around their position. That's why you do market and competitor analysis.

You Have Completed Step 3

In Step 3 you identified your industry and the trends in that industry.

You estimated the size of your markets and your probable share of those markets.

You learned who your competitors are and began to research their strong and weak points, to discover whether there is a place in the market for your business.

You revisited Personal Workshop #11, and re-evaluated your competitive edge in light of your more recent knowledge.

You finally determined whether or not your business idea makes good marketing sense. If the answer is NO, you have more work to do: rethink the idea, the product, services, and markets. You might even abandon an idea at this point and decide to start again from scratch with a new idea.

If the answer was YES, then you are ready to proceed to Step 4: Financial Analysis and determine whether or not your idea passes the final pre-venture feasibility barrier. Does it make good *financial* sense?

You Go Forward to Step 4 with the Following

Sources to help you determine your SIC code and industry trends

Personal Workshops to help you analyze your business idea in terms of its industry, target market, and competition

Information on market trends and life cycles

Information gathered from competitors to help you determine your competitive edge

---

Use this checklist to monitor your progress thus far in this guide. Check off those things you have completed. You may want to go back and complete any activities that you missed.

Step 3
Personal Checklist

❏ Determined what my industry is.

❏ Consulted reference books to locate trade information.

❏ Have determined where my industry is on the industry life cycle.

❏ Identified trends in my industry (Personal Workshop #13).

❏ Identified features and benefits of my product or service (Personal Workshop #14).

❏ Determined who my customers will be (Personal Workshop #15).

❏ Studied my competition and determined what my competitive edge will be (Personal Workshops #16, 17, and 18).

Step 4

Financial Analysis

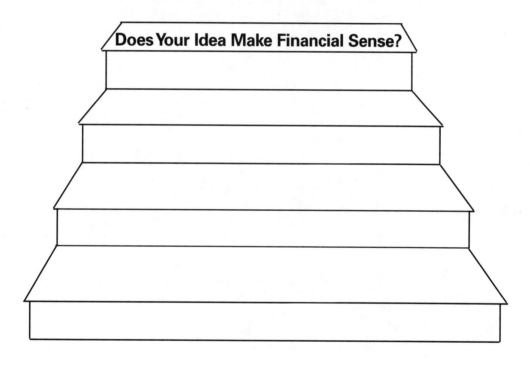

Does Your Idea Make Financial Sense?

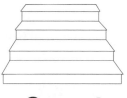

Step 4

Does Your Idea Make Financial Sense?

I never make small business loans. But I do make loans
to people who start small businesses.

—Norm Kent, former bank president,
1st NB of Portsmouth

You go into business to make money. If your business doesn't make money, that is, cover all of its expenses in a timely manner, it won't last long.

When you have completed Step 4, you will be able to:

• Arrive at a reasonable estimate of your start-up costs

• Set a preliminary operating budget

• Apply the break-even concept to your proposed business

• Learn where you might find start-up money

• Determine whether your business idea makes good financial sense

Why Financial Analysis Is Necessary

The most common single reason for small businesses to fail is running out of cash due to undercapitalization. A start-up business is **undercapitalized** if it does not have enough **capital** (cash plus available credit) to cover all of its start-up costs *plus* a cushion for expected losses during start-up. You can estimate these costs and requirements with a high degree of accuracy. These estimates aren't magic. They are just the result of the patient application of common sense to a series of questions captured in the forms later in this Step.

Don't guess at the capital requirements of your start-up. It's too risky.

Key Word

Two Types of Financial Feasibility

Capital

You have to have enough capital to get your business started. If you don't have enough cash and credit to get started right, you can't afford to be in business.

Operating Revenue

Key Word

Once you have started your business, it must generate enough cash to cover all of its expenses. In most cases that level of operating **revenue** takes time to develop, perhaps months. Accordingly, almost every business will need some extra funds to tide it over until operations chip in sufficient cash. You can figure out what you will probably need—and if you have that cushion (and feel you can afford to lose it if things don't work out), you can proceed forward confidently.

What's Included in the Financial Analysis?

- A detailed estimate, based on actual figures, of your start-up costs

- An operating budget for the first months of operations

- A break-even analysis to help you identify how many units you have to sell to cover all of your expenses

- A brief description of traditional start-up funding sources to give you an idea of where you might raise additional start-up capital (while this is not truly a part of your financial analysis, it will help you decide where to turn if you need more capital).

Use of Your Financial Analysis

Your financial analysis will spotlight weaknesses in the Concept and Customer areas that might otherwise pass unnoticed. An idea may appear to be strong, but once you run the numbers you may find that it turns out to be less profitable than you had hoped. Sometimes only minor adjustments to your plan will make it profitable—you will want to cut costs or market differently. But there are times when financial analysis shows that the basic

Key Note

> Many books on starting your own business will advise that you may not be able to take any salary for two to three years. If you figure your expenses this way, you might want to answer the question: Do I really want to start a business that doesn't generate a salary for two years?

idea has a fatal flaw, in which case you'd want to go back to the beginning. That's not a bad result from a financial analysis. You can always try again with a more promising idea.

More likely, you will find that you don't have enough cash on hand to meet your start-up costs and initial operating funds needs. In this case, you can scale your venture back, postpone it until you have enough cash to start it safely, or seek more cash from investors. But remember: If you cannot make a good case for the profitability of your venture, nobody will want to invest. (This includes you, since you are the person making the greatest investment.)

Your financial analysis is the last piece of your pre-venture feasibility analysis. If you conclude that your proposed business does make financial sense, your next step will be to write a business plan in which you examine the financial implications of your business idea in much greater detail.

For now, though, your purpose is only to answer the question, "Does my idea make good financial sense?" The three forms provided in the next Personal Workshop, backed up by an informal break-even analysis, give you a realistic way to answer the question.

Have a Detailed Estimate of Your Start-Up Costs

"Well begun is half-finished." If you start your business out on the right foot—which means with enough capital to get it up and running without being pinched for cash—your chances of success soar. Part of the puzzle involves start-up costs for initial inventories, leasehold improvements, licenses, and all the other one-time costs that you will incur when you start up your business.

You can hold some of these costs down by purchasing second-hand or borrowed equipment, renting space, and leasing equipment instead of purchasing. But the total amount will probably be more than you expect.

The dangers of undercapitalization cannot be too strongly emphasized. Get the real figures. If they are manageable, great. If not, perhaps you can find ways to lower them. Don't go ahead until you are pretty sure that you can afford to go into business.

Importance of Accuracy

It's important to be accurate, descriptive, and use **vendor** sources rather than guesstimates for start-up costs.

Key Word

The process of going over start-up costs again and again, looking for economies and ways to lower those costs, is excellent practice for actually running your business. Careful cash management is one of those business skills that spells the difference between success and failure.

You will be very accurate in projecting start-up costs if you speak with vendors, check out catalogs and price lists, and look for actual (as opposed to approximate) prices. Don't guess. A businesslike listing of assets will help you build credibility, especially if you can show that you have indeed done everything reasonable to hold costs down.

Accuracy also pays off when you sit down with your banker and explain why you need to borrow money for your start-up. That portion of the start-up costs that you pay for personally will show up as part of your investment in the business and can, on occasion, be used as collateral for a loan. Facts impress bankers. Guesses do not.

How do you know what it will cost to start your business? It is advisable to organize your start-up costs with the help of the forms in Personal Workshop #19. Before you work on the forms, see how Constance Fisk went about completing them.

 Constance has looked at three locations which she feels would be suitable for her business and has gone as far as discussing leases with the landlords. One of her criteria for selecting a location is that it should need little in the way of renovation.

Constance has some storage cabinets, but wants to add a few shelves for storage. She and her husband will build and install them so her investment is limited to materials. They will also build and install display stands, shelves, and tables.

She doesn't need a cash register or at least doesn't think she will. She does want to upgrade her computer and buy an accounting software package. That adds $1,200 to her start-up costs, but she expects this investment to pay for itself since she will do her own bookkeeping.

The phone system includes new lines and a stylish phone suitable for her upscale image.

The following table lists all of Constance's fixtures, furniture and equipment.

Part 1: List of Furniture, Fixtures, and Equipment

Leave out or add items to suit your business. Use separate sheets to list exactly what you need for each of the items below.	If you plan to pay cash in full, enter the full amount below and in the last column.	If you are going to pay by installments, enter in the down payment plus installments for 3 months.	Estimate of the cash you need for furniture, fixtures, and equipment.
Counters			
Storage shelves, cabinets	500		
Display stands, shelves, tables	1,500		
Cash register			
Computers and software	1,200		
Communications equipment (phone systems, fax)	500		
Copiers			
Safe			
Window display fixtures			
Special lighting			
Outside signage	700		
Delivery equipment	1,600		
Other (specify)	400		
Total: Furniture, Fixtures, Equipment. Enter under Part 1: Starting costs you only have to pay once.	6,400		6,400

Signage is regulated by zoning, so instead of a sign she will have a local artist paint her name (Bridal Elegance) and an appropriate design on the glass door and on the display window.

Decorating and remodeling costs are primarily for cleaning and some painting. If Constance had not selected sites with renovation costs in mind, this might have been substantially higher.

She and her husband will install the equipment themselves; she has $4,800 of sewing and cutting equipment. See her personal financial statement in Step 1.

As an extension of her part-time business, Constance has some inventory on hand.

Deposits, legal and accounting fees, licenses and permits, and opening promotional costs are straightforward: she made some phone calls.

Her cash cushion (working capital) is a guess, based on her experience.

The total estimated cash she needs is $11,800. She has some cash on hand ($3,750) and might borrow against the education fund for more cash. The $4,800 in equipment will be part of her investment in her business.

What is Your Operating Budget?

Key Word

You don't have to become an accountant to understand and use a budget. In fact, you are already familiar with budgeting from handling your personal finances. All your **operating budget** does is set down the expected amounts and timing of revenues and expenses in a standard form that can be used to strengthen your business decisions.

Your operating budget serves a variety of purposes. It helps you hold down spending, provides and supports financial self-discipline, and helps you set timelines and measurable goals. It gives you a scorecard, a way of seeing how well you are doing and whether or not you need to change some business behaviors. It is an indispensable tool for raising cash, whether from bankers, vendors or investors. It provides a reality check: will your business expenses outrun the business's ability to generate revenue?

The Appropriate Time Frame for Your Operating Budget

Key Word

Operating budgets cover a period of time, usually a **fiscal year** (required for tax purposes) but are most useful if broken down to a monthly or even weekly basis.

Key Note

Your cash cushion really represents your tolerance for risk. The greater your tolerance, the less cash cushion you will probably place in this category.

Part 2: Start-Up Costs You Only Have to Pay Once

Fixtures and equipment	$6,400	XXXXXXXX	Put the total from Part 1 here
Decorating and remodeling	1,200	XXXXXXXX	Speak with contractor
Installation of fixtures and equipment	- 0 -	XXXXXXXX	Talk to suppliers from whom you buy these
Starting inventory	1,000	XXXXXXXX	Ask suppliers
Deposits for public utilities	300	XXXXXXXX	Ask utility companies
Legal and other professional fees	500	XXXXXXXX	Ask lawyer, accountant, etc.
Licenses and permits	50	XXXXXXXX	Find out from city offices
Advertising and promotion for opening	850	XXXXXXXX	Estimate: ask ad agencies
Accounts receivable		XXXXXXXX	What you will need to buy more stock until credit customers pay
Cash	1,500	XXXXXXXX	For unexpected expenses, losses, special purchases, etc.
Other (specify)		XXXXXXXX	Make a separate list and enter total
Total Estimated Cash you Need to Start:	11,800	XXXXXXXX	Add up all the numbers in column 1

Most businesses will find that a monthly budget is the most useful, as it allows enough time to smooth out some of the bumps, yet is short enough so that if you find something going wrong (or going better than you expected) you can take timely action. Information that is 12 months old can arrive too late to do you much good, especially during the early months of a start-up when reliable patterns haven't been established.

Ask your SBDC counselor or other financial advisor for advice on this.

Constance thinks a salary of $24,000 a year would be about right for her as the manager. Her social security payments (known as self-employment tax) will be about $300 per month (this is based on 15 percent of her salary). Note that this does not include any of her estimated income taxes (federal or state), unemployment compensation, or workers compensation (because she has not incorporated and does not have any additional employees). These do vary from state to state. For information regarding your state, contact your state employment department.

The total of $4,220 in expenses per month will be used in the next section, break-even analysis, to make Constance Fisk's decision about the financial feasibility of this venture. At this stage it looks very promising; her expenses annualize to $50,640 (or 12 times the monthly figure), while she thinks she will be able to sell about $60,000 worth of product and service.

Remember that Constance is estimating a salary of $2,000 per month. Because she is the owner of the business she will be paid **only after all other bills are paid**. Therefore, if she does not sell the 2.5 dresses per month that she is estimating, her salary may be less than the $2,000 per month. Keep this in mind when you determine the "cushion" necessary to start the business.

Break-Even Analysis

Key Word

Your **break-even point** is defined as the level of sales at which you don't make a **profit** and don't suffer a loss. If you sell less than this level, you lose money; sell more and make a profit.

Break-even analysis is a great reality check. If you know that you have to have sales of $100,000 to reach break-even, but have estimated most likely sales at $50,000 it sends a clear and strong signal.

Key Note

Starting a new business may be time dependent. That is, if your business has periods of peaks and valleys (most do), your starting date may determine how much money you actually need for cushion or start-up.

Part 3: Operating Budget

Item	Monthly Expenses Column 1	Annual Expenses Column 2
Salary of owner or manager	$2,000	$24,000
All other salaries and wages	None at this time	
Rent or mortgage	600	7,200
Advertising	400	4,800
Delivery expense	- 0 -	- 0 -
Supplies/materials	500	6,000
Telephone/fax	100	1,200
Utilities	150	1,800
Insurance	70	840
Taxes (Social Security only)	300	3,600
Interest	No Loan	
Loan payments	No Loan	
Maintenance	75	900
Professional Fees	25	300
Miscellaneous		
Other (specify)		
Total Costs	$4,220	$50,640

Personal Workshop Preparation #19: Estimated Start-Up Costs and Operating Budget

Use the following forms in Personal Workshop #19 to organize your start-up costs and to determine your operating budget. You may want to refer back to how Constance Fisk completed these forms.

Personal Notes

_____

_____

_____

THE PURPOSE OF THIS WORKSHOP IS TO ESTIMATE YOUR START-UP COSTS AND OPERATING BUDGET

Personal Workshop #19

Estimated Start-Up Costs and Operating Budget

Part 1: List of Furniture, Fixtures, and Equipment

Leave out or add items to suit your business. Use separate sheets to list exactly what you need for each of the items below.	If you plan to pay cash in full, enter the full amount below and in the last column.	If you are going to pay by installments, enter in the down payment plus installments for 3 months.	Estimate of the cash you need for furniture, fixtures, and equipment.
Counters			
Storage shelves, cabinets			
Display stands, shelves, tables			
Cash register			
Computers and software			
Communications equipment (phone systems, fax)			
Copiers			
Safe			
Window display fixtures			
Special lighting			
Outside signage			
Delivery equipment			
Other (specify)			
Total: Furniture, Fixtures, Equipment. Enter under Part 1: Starting costs you only have to pay once.			

Part 2: Start-Up Costs You Only Have to Pay Once

Fixtures and equipment		XXXXXXXX	Put the total from Part 1 here
Decorating and remodeling		XXXXXXXX	Speak with contractor
Installation of fixtures and equipment		XXXXXXXX	Talk to suppliers from whom you buy these
Starting inventory		XXXXXXXX	Ask suppliers
Deposits for public utilities		XXXXXXXX	Ask utility companies
Legal and other professional fees		XXXXXXXX	Ask lawyer, accountant, etc.
Licenses and permits		XXXXXXXX	Find out from city offices
Advertising and promotion for opening		XXXXXXXX	Estimate: ask ad agencies
Accounts receivable		XXXXXXXX	What you will need to buy more stock until credit customers pay
Cash		XXXXXXXX	For unexpected expenses, losses, special purchases, etc.
Other (specify)		XXXXXXXX	Make a separate list and enter total
Total Estimated Cash you Need to Start:		XXXXXXXX	Add up all the numbers in column 1

Part 3: Operating Budget

Item	Monthly Expenses Column 1	Annual Expenses Column 2
Salary of owner or manager		
All other salaries and wages		
Rent or mortgage		
Advertising		
Delivery expense		
Supplies/materials		
Telephone/fax		
Utilities		
Insurance		
Taxes (Social Security only)		
Interest		
Loan payments		
Maintenance		
Professional Fees		
Miscellaneous		
Other (specify)		
Total Costs		

How to Compute a Basic Break-Even Point

The break-even point can be expressed mathematically. The formula is:

Break-even Point (units) = Fixed Costs / (Selling Price - Unit Variable Cost)

 Break-even points can be calculated for various time periods (yearly, monthly, weekly, or even daily). Because Constance has just estimated her monthly operating costs, it is possible to calculate her monthly break-even point. This can be shown as follows:

Key Word

1. Calculate fixed costs: **Fixed costs** are those that stay the same no matter what level sales are. For Constance, these include all of her monthly operating costs *except* her raw materials and supplies. That is:

$4,220 minus $500 = $3,720.

2. Estimate average selling price: Recall that Constance estimated that her average sale will be $2,000.

Key Word

3. Calculate unit variable costs: These are the costs that will vary *directly* with sales. For Constance, the only costs which meet this requirement are her materials and supplies, which she estimates will be $500 per month. (It is important to note that her variable cost ratio is not typical, primarily because she does not have hourly employees.) Earlier Constance estimated that she would serve about 30 brides per year, or an average of 2.5 per month. Her unit variable costs will be:

$$\$500 / 2.5 = \$200.$$

4. Calculate break-even point: Plugging these numbers into the formula, her break-even point in units will be:

$$\$3,720 / (\$2,000 - \$200) = 2.07 \text{ weddings per month}$$

This could be rounded to 2.0 weddings per month.

5. Convert to dollars: If she wanted to, Constance could convert the break-even point she just calculated to a dollar figure, simply by multiplying 2.07 times $2,000 (the average unit selling price).

Her break-even point is $4,140 per month.

Shortcomings of Break-Even Analysis

Since break-even rests on the relationship between fixed and variable expenses, you have to have a pretty good idea of what these will be and a reasonably accurate sales forecast as well. In a start-up, this may look like a tall order, but remember that you don't have to know everything—you just have to know where to find people who have the knowledge you need. Financial analysis such as break-even is one of those places.

How Many Bowls of Soup?

One way to test the reality of your sales forecasts is to express it in units which make sense for your business. How many hours of consulting work, or how many haircuts, or how many bowls of soup does that total represent? Can you bill that many hours, or provide that number of haircuts, or serve that many bowls of soup?

Constance has calculated that the average wedding will result in $2,000 of revenue, based on her experience and on her research. Her break-even point of two weddings per month works out to about $4,100 in monthly sales, or about $49,000 per year.

Since she has already figured out that she will average 2.5 weddings per month, this gives Constance a cushion of only about a half a wedding per month. The wedding business is quite seasonal. It would seem likely for her to have considerably more weddings than her average May through October and fewer from November through April. Constance must be prepared for this variation.

Another way to look at it is that Constance will have to reach 80 percent of her sales forecast (monthly or yearly) before she will start to make a profit. Many business owners would not feel comfortable with a margin for error that is this small. *At this level of analysis*, her plan appears to make pretty good financial sense. Her financial risks will be small, which a banker will take into consideration should Constance choose to finance her business with a loan.

The beauty of B/E is that, given the basic formulas, you can express your business's break-even in terms of units sold, numbers of customers, or similar familiar quantities. One example is that of the owner of a small restaurant who figured his B/E in terms of bowls of soup he needed to sell per day. He discovered that his restaurant couldn't serve enough customers even during his peak periods to come close to B/E, so he changed his marketing strategy to a highly profitable luncheon take-out and delivery operation.

It is useful to know your break-even when planning and actually operating your business. The break-even point establishes a target or a minimum by which to gauge your progress. But break-even is only one of many analysis tools that successful entrepreneurs use to help them run their businesses.

Personal Workshop Preparation #20: Is it Right for Me?

You have taken four steps closer to having a business of your own. You are now ready to complete the next and final Personal Workshop to determine if your business idea passes the feasibility test.

Personal Workshop #20
Is It Right for Me?

Does My Idea Make:

Personal Sense?	Yes	No
Business Sense?	Yes	No
Marketing Sense?	Yes	No
Financial Sense?	Yes	No

You Have Completed Step 4

This completes the fourth and final step of your start-up feasibility analysis.

You have estimated your start-up costs, including one-time costs, and compared the total to your free or liquid assets to see if you can realistically afford to start up your business.

You have set up an operating budget, which listed your monthly expenses, based on your projected sales.

You performed a rudimentary break-even analysis to see if your proposed business makes good financial sense, and have expressed that dollar amount in "bowls of soup" or other units that make sense for your business idea.

Finally, you have determined whether or not your business passes all of the feasibility barriers: Does it make good **Personal sense? Business sense? Marketing sense? Financial sense?** If the answer to these four questions is YES, then you are ready to take the next steps towards starting your own business.

You Go Forward with the Following

 Instructions on how to apply the break-even concept to your proposed business.

Forms to help you determine your estimated start-up costs and operating budget.

Sources to contact for assistance with financial questions and concerns.

Use this checklist to monitor your progress thus far in this guide. Check off those things you have completed. You may want to go back and complete any activities that you missed.

Step 4

Personal Checklist

❏ Determined what my estimated start-up costs will be (Personal Workshop #19).

❏ Set a preliminary operating budget (Personal Workshop #19).

❏ Did a break-even analysis to determine how much I need to sell.

❏ Answered the 4 important questions to determine if my business idea will work (Personal Workshop #20).

The Next Step

A Business Plan

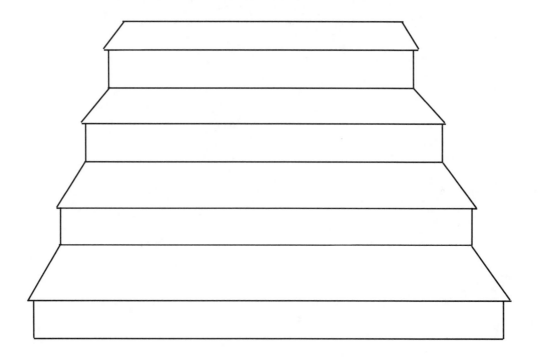

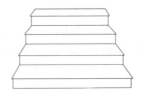

The Next Step

A Business Plan

After completing this guide and deciding that your business idea is a good one, your next step will be to write a business plan. A business plan is a short, written document which explains what your business is going to be, who the markets for its products will be, how much that market will be satisfied, and why the business will be successful.

A business plan, a document consisting of approximately 20 pages, including financial statements, is more than adequate for most small businesses. There will be exceptions, but they are rare, and your advisors will help you determine whether or not you need to go to a longer format.

Business plans are commonly required by banks and other investors. The larger the business financing needs, the more important the plan becomes as a financing tool. A more pressing reason for writing a careful, detailed business plan is that it is a way to make a model of the business that you can use to test out ideas inexpensively. Your feasibility analysis in the pre-venture curriculum is a start. The business plan takes that feasibility analysis much further, going into how the plan will be implemented, who and when to hire employees or take on other investors—and so on. Your business plan is cheap insurance against avoidable errors. It serves well as a communications tool and as a financing proposal.

A suggested format for your business plan follows:

I. Executive Summary

A short statement of what the plan is about. You may be using it to raise cash from investors or a bank, in which case you will have to show prospective investors why their investment makes good sense for them.

II. The Business

- Description of the business
- Product or service
- Market
- Competition
- Operations (how the product or service will be provided)
- Personnel
- Management

III. Financial Statements

- Sales forecast
- Income statements
- Cash flow statements
- Break-even analysis
- Balance sheet
- Historical financials (if any)

IV. Appendices

These depend on the nature of your venture, and may include resumes of management, letters of commitment, legal material, brochures or other promotional materials, and other material which substantiates your claims.

There are many sources of information and assistance for writing a business plan. The best source is your Small Business Development Center. They have plenty of experience helping people in this process. In addition, they

Key Note

If you're interested in financing options at this stage, wait! All institutions require a business plan prior to lending money. Even if you do not need outside financing, you really must have a business plan before you start.

have workshops which help you through the planning process and books and other resources to make the task manageable.

Sources of Financing:
Where Do You Find Money for a Start-Up?

Seventy-three percent of start-ups are financed with owner savings or loans from family and friends (F&F). The majority of the rest are started with a combination of owner savings, F&F, and bank financing. A few use other sources of capital such as credit card advances, "asset based lenders" such as Household Finance or Beneficial, advance payments from customers, vendor credit, or government-backed loans of various kinds. A very few get investment money from "angels" (rich private investors), venture capitalists, or sale of stock.

Unless you have a very unusual situation, you will have to provide most of the seed money yourself. While there are exceptions, they are rare; most investors will demand that your personal assets be on the line before they will put their assets into your business.

Each of the following financing sources has its own pros and cons. Use your judgment.

Financing Options

Personal Savings. Look at your personal financial statement, the one you filled out in Step 2. The advantage of using your personal savings is that you don't have to persuade anyone that your idea is a good one. It's fast. The disadvantage is that you might lose your investment.

Your most immediate sources of cash are:

- Checking and saving accounts, certificates of deposit, sale of stocks and bonds, sale of real estate or other investments, profit-sharing or retirement funds from previous job.

Key Note

Service businesses have relatively low start-up costs. Retail and manufacturing businesses have relatively high initial costs. If you are strapped for cash, this could affect your choice of a business to enter. More importantly, if you have a limited amount of cash to invest, you want to make sure that you can not only cover start-up costs but also have enough capital left to run the business until such time as it can support itself on its operating revenues. Getting started is just the beginning.

- Loans: You can borrow against assets such as stocks and bonds, re-mortgage real estate, take out a second mortgage or home equity loan, credit card advances, borrow against cash value of life insurance.

- Look at your other assets (cars, boats, antiques, collections, jewelry and so forth) which might be sold or put up as collateral for a loan.

- Consider taking a part-time job or moonlighting to raise extra cash.

There is no way you can start a business without investing your own savings and other assets.

Family & Friends (F&F) may be willing to invest money in your proposed business, either as equity (a share of the business) or as a loan.

Investors want to know whether or not a person believes strongly enough in an idea to involve friends and family. If the answer is no, they won't invest a dime.

The downside of F&F money is that there may be emotional entanglements, loss of money, and consequent loss of friends. Keep the proposition businesslike and it will probably work out.

F&F are also potential co-signers or collateral providers for loans.

Remember, the co-signer is really the one taking the risk.

Partners can be a great source of start-up capital and can bring a lot more than money to the table. Some start-ups work best with a team approach— say a good salesperson, a clever engineer, and an administrator.

The pros and cons of having a partner are about evenly balanced. On the plus side, you'll have an ally who is as committed to the business as you are, with extra assets to invest, and with skills to augment yours. On the down side, you'll have to share any profits, and if things don't work out, shedding a business partner can be even more disagreeable than getting divorced.

The moral: Take on a partner only with great care— and a commercial version of a prenuptial agreement.

Loans are a major source of funds for start-up companies. The down side of any loan is that borrowing is expensive.

- Most banks will make personal loans to individuals who have been their customers and who have a good credit rating. Commercial banks are major lenders to the small business community, but do not usually lend to start-up businesses. Bank loans which are guaranteed in part by the SBA often make it easier for a clearly conceived start-up to get bank financing.

- Credit unions, S&Ls, and co-operative banks all lend to small businesses and may be more receptive to your start-up than commercial banks.

- Direct SBA loans are hard to get, but for some start-ups, especially those that meet their MicroLoan Program or other targeted loan programs, are an excellent source of funds. Check with the SBA.

- Trade credit is not easily gained by a start-up. Once your business has established a track record, trade credit becomes one of the two major funding sources for most small businesses. The other is retained operating earnings.

- If you have customers lined up, you might be able to induce them to pre-pay for your goods and services.

- Commercial credit companies such as Household Finance and Beneficial are another funding source worth investigating. They can take greater risks than a commercial bank and are much more likely to fund start-ups. The drawback is that you will pay a substantially higher rate of interest than a bank would charge.

Equity investors other than friends and family are hard to attract. If your business has explosive growth potential, your banker and other financial advisors will steer you in this direction. Otherwise, don't waste your time or theirs by pursuing the mythical and elusive "Other People's Money."

- Private investors ("angels") are rich folk who invest primarily in local businesses that they know something about. On the plus side, if they have an interest in your business they can provide more than money. They'll be actively involved, give advice, make referrals and so on. On the minus side, ditto. They can get in the way.

- The improbable: venture capitalists, investment bankers, insurance companies, pension funds, etc. These players invest major amounts of money and look for fantastic rates of return. Almost no small start-up meets their criteria.

- SBICs (Small Business Investment Companies) and MESBICs (Minority Enterprise SBICs) provide a special kind of venture capital. They invest in businesses which will provide substantial employment opportunities, primarily in low- to medium-tech companies. Check with the SBA for current standards and a list of SBICs in your area.

- State and local economic development agencies sometimes have capital available for certain start-ups. Ask; but don't be surprised if their standards and requirements are extremely difficult to meet.

Sale of stock is possible but improbable for most start-ups and an expensive way to raise money due to legal fees and filing requirements.

Ten Things Bankers Look for in a Loan Application

To help you get the capital you need to build your business, here are ten things bankers look for in a loan application.

1. Every banker rates *applicants* (not applications) by the "5Cs of Credit." As a banker told the applicant as he handed over a check, "I never make loans to small businesses. Just to small-business owners."

Character: What sort of person are you? What is your track record, your credit history?

Calacity: How much can you safely borrow?

Capital: How much of your own money is at risk—and is it enough to provide a cushion for the bank? Is it enough so that this loan, with your invested capital, will help your business to prosper?

Conditions: What are the prevailing and anticipated economic and competitive conditions? Is the economy you work in getting stronger, weaker, or remaining the same? Is the industry you are in thriving, stuttering, or shrinking?

Collateral: What hard assets can you back up a loan with? Bankers don't take collateral because they want to be in the second-hand equipment or house business—they know that if you have assets at risk you will stick to your business if and when things go wrong.

2. How much cash do you want? Be specific. Don't ask for more than you need or less. If you aren't sure, explain the need to your banker and ask for help.

3. What are you going to do with the money? What is the business purpose of the loan? To buy inventory or equipment, or expand, or . . . .

4. Why will this loan be a good thing for your business? Business loans have to make your business stronger. Again, be specific: improve productivity, enter a new market, stock seasonal inventory, provide capital. . . .

5. Why do you need our depositor's money to do it? While banks are in the business of renting money to borrowers, they have to know why you cannot fund the loan from operating profits or from your own investment or backers.

6. When will you pay the loan back? The longer the term, the greater the risk perceived by the bank. Normally, short-term (under one year) loans fund one inventory turn or season: equipment loans and working capital loans take one to five years to repay; and long-term loans (mortgages, for example) can take up to 15 years.

7. How will you pay it back? Short-term loans get paid out of an inventory turn or seasonal profits. Equipment or other mid- to long-term loans are repaid from operating profit. Be prepared to show your cash flow and balance sheet projections to support a loan request; these help show the banker the details of your repayment plan.

8. What happens if things do not work out as planned? A contingency plan is frequently requested, especially of small borrowers. In it you lay out what happens in a worst-case scenario. Remember, the banker's first concern is being repaid.

9. What happens if you start growing fast? This is the flip side of the worst-case scenario. Fast growth devours capital and stops cash flow dead in its tracks. What will you do if your business really takes off?

10. Who are your customers? The most critical question of all. Small business owners are traditionally overly optimistic about their ability to generate business. Bankers want more than hopes and hunches. They want—and need—facts about your market, your market share or position, and how you will attract and retain customers.

You need to know the answers to these questions yourself. Even if you aren't planning to borrow money you have to have the answers to these questions ready at all times. It's only prudent business management.

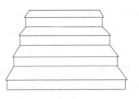

Epilogue

Where Are the Case Study Entrepreneurs Today?

You have followed seven case study entrepreneurs as they have taken four smart steps in the process of testing their business ideas. Where are these people today?

Constance Fisk went ahead with her business, got her bank loan, leasing second-floor space in an upscale retail building. Her projections turned out to be conservative: the first year she worked with 25 weddings, but they averaged nearly $4,000 apiece. As a result, she was able to hire an assistant and looks forward to next year with confidence.

Ellen Redfern's decision to work for someone else for a while was a good one. She still hopes to open a business of her own one day. Her experiences in researching business opportunities and seeing if they fit her have whetted her appetite for independence. She still hasn't found the right opportunity for her, but she's looking. Her latest project, begun part-time, is a newsletter for teachers in adult education.

Dave Campbell started his wine store on a shoestring, a mistake he says he wouldn't repeat since it has severely limited the growth of his business. After two full years in business he is finally beginning to make a decent living and taking some time off.

Dennis Aney started his business, DCA Manufacturing Inc., and almost reached his break-even point for the first year of operation. He expects to be profitable by the end of his second year. Dennis has four full-time employees and a nice production facility located in a former cheese plant. He was fortunate to find his first major customer right in his backyard. Although he has hired manufacturer's reps to do most of his selling, Dennis has found it critical to get out and make sales calls himself.

 Thorndike Press, Phillip Treleven's large-print business, continues to prosper. His early grasp of what the market really wanted (both the readers and the librarians who do the buying of most large-print books) has paid off in fast, profitable growth in a tough industry.

 The Sandlers went ahead with their Bed & Breakfast and have learned to do well in a crowded market by taking a business-like approach to their markets. Unlike most of their competitors, they actively seek business and don't rely on passive advertising to do the trick. Dick Sandler still works full-time while Ruth runs the B&B—but if their occupancy rate continues to be as strong as it has been for the past two years (100 percent in the busy tourist season, over 60 percent during the slack season) they will add a wing to their building and Dick will retire to help Ruth run what will become an inn.

 Laura Cleminson is still working full-time while pursuing her design business on a part-time basis. She is making up for a lack of capital by going ahead slowly, growing a reputation for her designs, learning how to deal with manufacturers and store buyers, and making contacts in the industry. She says that this slow pace is very beneficial, as she is finding out how the industry really works without expensive learning-by-blunder. She still plans to start her business, but won't leap in until she has accumulated enough capital and experience to feel that the time is right.

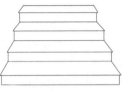

Appendix

Networking Tips

Networking skills can be learned. Practice these tips before going to a networking function and you will be pleasantly surprised at how easy and valuable networking can be.

1. Decide in advance what you want to get out of the networking function. It's wise to have an individual goal for each event. Some possible goals are:

   - Learn how three new businesses operate

   - Find a woman with a business similar to yours

   - Meet and get business cards from five prospective customers

   - Spend at least five minutes with someone you've wanted to meet so that she or he knows who you are and what you do.

2. Prepare, prepare, prepare. Think of opening lines like "What business are you in?" Then think of at least five more questions that will help you attain your networking goals:

   - How long have you been in business?

   - How did you get into that business?

   - I'm not familiar with your business. Tell me about it!

   - What do you like best about your business?

   - That sounds like a problem I have. Could we meet for lunch next week and talk about it?

3. Be professional. Dress and act appropriately. "Hello, I'm Laura Cleminson" will get a conversation going. Keep in mind that networking functions are not the place to close a sale, but rather to meet other business people.

4. Follow up appropriately. Send a thank-you note to anyone who steers business your way or gives you especially valuable information or ideas. Call people you met and ask for a chance to make a formal sales presentation. Arrange to meet for lunch or coffee. Send clippings of articles that you think would be of interest to them. Even if they have already read it they'll be pleased.

5. Nurture the relationship. Always close the loop. People love to help other people and feel needed and useful. Keep them informed about what you're up to, tell them how you applied their suggestions.

Go to the meetings, follow up with people you meet, and develop the relationships. You will be amazed at how much of a difference it will make in your business and in your life.

(Adapted with permission of the author and publisher from *On Your Own,* © 1990 by Laurie B. Zuckerman, Upstart Publishing Co., see pp. 6-7.)

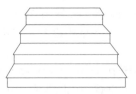

Key Resources

Books

Upstart Publishing Company, a division of Dearborn Publishing Group, Chicago, IL. Call 800-235-8866 for a free catalog. List of titles include:

Launching New Ventures: An Entrepreneurial Approach, Kathleen Allen, 1995. Innovative entrepreneurship text that enables the students to plan and start a world-class venture guide that takes the reader from the first basic steps of developing an idea to creating a detailed business and marketing plan. Instructor's manual available. 496 pp., $35.00

Strategic Planning for the New and Small Business, Fred L. Fry and Charles R. Stoner, 1995. This highly practical text guides students through the strategic planning process using case histories and examples of actual businesses. Unique in that it is a strategy book aimed specifically at small businesses. Instructor's manual available. 256 pp., $24.95

Financial Essentials for Small Business Success, Joseph Tabet and Jeffrey Slater, 1994. This text stresses the importance of common sense in overcoming the problems of poor record keeping and planning. Step-by-step guidance results in students learning to interpret financial reports and building the necessary financial tools for a profitable small business. Instructor's manual available. 272 pp., $22.95

Business Planning Guide, Seventh Edition, David H. Bangs, Jr., 1995. Designed for both beginning students and more experienced practitioners, this is a vital tool for putting together a complete and effective business plan and financing proposal. Contains three complete sample business plans. Available on CD-ROM. Instructor's manual available. 224 pp., $22.95

Anatomy of a Business Plan, Third Edition, Linda Pinson and Jerry Jinnett, 1996. The step-by-step approach assumes no prior knowledge of a business plan. This basic presentation enables the student or entrepreneur to prepare a start-up plan for a new small business or plan new strategies for an existing business. Instructor's manual available. 272 pp., $22.95

Market Planning Guide, Fourth Edition, David H. Bangs, Jr., 1995. Practical text that shows students how to create an effective marketing plan suited to the business' goals and resources. Features complete marketing plans for two actual businesses. Instructor's manual available. 257 pp., $22.95

Target Marketing, Second Edition, Linda Pinson and Jerry Jinnett, 1996. Text is a comprehensive guide to developing a marketing plan for your business. Broken into a simple three-stage marketing process of research, reach and retain. Instructor's manual available. 176 pp., $22.95

The Start Up Guide, David H. Bangs, Jr., 1994. Walks students through every phase of small business start-up. Text is based on a hypothetical one-year process. 176 pp., $22.95

Steps to Small Business Start-Up, Linda Pinson and Jerry Jinnett, 1993. One step at a time, the student learns the mechanics of business start-ups and gets started on everything from record-keeping, marketing and business planning. Contains forms, examples and worksheets. Instructor's manual available. 255 pp., $22.95

Cash Flow Control Guide, David H. Bangs, Jr., 1990. Step by step guide to learning a cash flow control process for the small business. It uses a real-life example of a company that demonstrates how cash flow planning can smooth out some of the small business's roughest spots. 88 pp., $19.95

Keeping the Books, Linda Pinson and Jerry Jinnett, 1993. Hands-on introduction to small business bookkeeping, which may be used with students who have no financial or accounting background. It covers all the essentials and provides numerous sample forms and worksheets. Instructor's manual available. New edition: Spring 1996. 208 pp., $22.95

Export Profits, Jack Wolf, 1993. Comprehensive guide that simplifies the complex subject of exporting. It assumes no prior knowledge of international trade and with the aid of resources, examples and sample documents, covers all the aspects of exporting. 304 pp., $22.95

Cases in Small Business Management, John de Young, 1994. More than 50 intriguing and useful case studies focusing on typical problems faced by small business managers every day. Problem solving is encouraged through end-of-chapter questions that lead students through an analysis of possible solutions. Instructor's manual available. 288 pp., $24.95

Problems and Solutions in Small Business Management, Editors of Forum, 1995. A collection of case studies selected by the editors of the small business journal, *Forum*. A problem drawn from an actual business is presented and then followed by three possible solutions written by experts from a variety of areas within the field of small business management. 192 pp., $22.95

Other Titles

Small Business Source Book, Detroit, Michigan: Gale Research Co., 1995.

The Brass Tacks Entrepreneur, by Jim Schell. New York: Henry Holt and Company, Inc. 1993.

Magazines

Black Enterprise, 130 5th Avenue, 10th Floor, New York, NY 10011-4399. (212) 242-8000.

D&B Reports, 299 Park Avenue, New York, NY 10171. (212) 593-6724.

Entrepreneur Magazine, 2392 Morse Avenue, Irvine, CA 92714-6234.

In Business, J.G. Press, Inc., 419 State Street, Emmaus, PA 18049-0351. (215) 967-4135.

Inc. Magazine, Goldhirsch Group, 38 Commercial Wharf, Boston, MA 02110-3809. (617) 248-8000.

Small Business Forum, University of Wisconsin-Extension, Madison, WI 53706-1498. (608) 263-7843.

Associations

American Society of Independent Business, 777 Main Street, Suite 1600, Fort Worth, TX 76102. (817) 870-1880.

National Association for the Cottage Industry, Box 14850, Chicago, IL 60614-0850. (312) 472-8116.

National Association for the Self-Employed, 2328 Gravel Road, Fort Worth, TX 76118. (800) 232-6273.

National Small Business Association, 1155 15th Street NW, Washington, DC 20005-2706. (202) 293-8830.

On-Line Services

America Online (AOL):. Call 800-827-6364 for a free trial membership.

CompuServe: Call 800-487-0588 for a free trial membership.

Prodigy: Call 1-800-PRODIGY ext. 358 for a free trial membership.

Local

SBDC: Contact your local Small Business Development Center for local publications.

Library

Check with your librarian for resource recommendations.

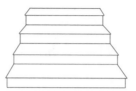

Key Word Glossary

Assets   The valuable resources or properties and property rights owned by the company. Included might be cash, inventory, equipment, and buildings.-

Break-even point   The level of sales where profits made from sales equal total costs and expenses.

Capital   Money and other assets you would use to start up a business; ownership.

Collateral   Securities, evidence of deposit, or other property pledged by a borrower to secure repayment of a loan.

Competition   Business rival for customers or markets. Any company that sells a similar product or service to the same people you want to sell to.

Demographics   The statistical study of human populations, especially with reference to size and density, distribution, and vital statistics.

Equity   Equity is the owner's investment in the business. Unlike capital, equity is what remains after the liabilities of the company are subtracted from the assets—thus it may be greater or less than the capital invested in the business. Equity investment carries with it a share of ownership and usually a share in the profits, as well as some say in how the business is managed.

Expenditures   How much you spend.

Financial statements   Documents that show your financial situation.

Fiscal year   A 12-month period between settlements of financial accounts.

Fixed costs   Expenses which do not vary with the level of sales, such as loan payments, rent, and salaries.

Liabilities   Money that you owe.

Marketing   Creating customers; the process of planning and executing the conception, pricing, promotion, and distribution of ideas, goods, and services to satisfy individual and organizational objectives.

Market niche   A targeted market segment that you determine is not adequately being served by the current competition.

Operating budget   Amount you have budgeted to actually run your business.

Profit   Total revenue minus total expenditures.

Psychographics   Used to segment markets. Psychographics is the study of the psychological profiles of individuals. For example, "early adopters" (people who like to be the first to buy something new) have a very different profile from "survivors," people who are barely scraping by and are loathe to buy anything that isn't totally familiar to them.

Revenue   An amount of money regularly coming in.

Segmentation   Defining your potential customers by various characteristics such as geographics, demographics, purchasing habits, or lifestyles.

Target market   A group of people with common needs, the most likely potential customers for your business.

Undercapitalization   Providing too little capital for the successful operation of the business.

Variable costs   Expenses that fluctuate based on the amount of sales.

Vendors   Suppliers of goods and services to your business.

Personal Workshops

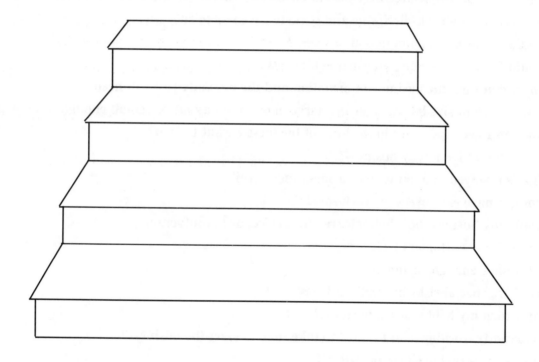

Personal Workshop #1
What's In It for Me?

Smart Steps is designed to help you find answers to the many questions you will be asking as you develop a business idea. Use this workshop to help you identify those questions that are relevant to you. Place a check before those questions that you want answered as you complete this guide.

❑ **How can I be sure that my decision to go into business makes sense for me?**

❑ **How can I find the right business for me?**

❑ **How will being in business affect my family?**

❑ **What kinds of people are successful in business ownership? Am I one of those?**

❑ **Do I have enough self-discipline and stick-to-itiveness to succeed?**

❑ **Should I consider a home-based business?**

❑ **Should I consider buying an existing business?**

❑ **Where can I get the business information and the help/advice I will need?**

❑ **Is there a right size business for me, large enough to pay off but small enough to manage?**

❑ **How can I get experience in the kind of business I want to own?**

❑ **When should I start my business?**

❑ **What's involved in making my business successful?**

❑ **Should I have employees or work solo?**

❑ **Should my business be wholesale, retail, service, or manufacturing?**

❑ **Who will my customers be?**

❑ **Will I have enough customers?**

❑ **Are there special risks in small business?**

❑ **Can I turn my hobby into a business?**

❑ **If currently working, can I afford to take time to start the business?**

❑ **Can I start a real business part-time?**

❑ **How much cash will it take me to start my business?**

❑ **How and where can I get financing?**

❑ **Do I need to know a lot of financial information to succeed?**

❑ **What would happen if I were to fail?**

❑ _____

❑ _____

THE PURPOSE OF THIS WORKSHOP IS TO FORM AN IMAGE OF THE BUSINESS YOU WANT TO BE IN

Personal Workshop #2
Through the Keyhole

Have you ever said to yourself, "I can see myself running *that* business?"

Picture yourself in a business of your own. You might be making pottery, setting up a factory to produce salsa, distributing wooden furniture, running a fancy restaurant, or helping someone solve an interior design problem. Or whatever. Let your imagination loose.

Make your vision come alive. Talk about it, write about it, or draw it. What are you wearing? What are you doing? Are you in front of customers? Working alone? Working at home? Do you need a computer, a store, or a bulldozer?

You'll want to come back to this image again and again. It will probably change, maybe completely, as your ideas take firmer shape. But for now, just try to imagine what it will be like in your own business.

Personal Workshop #3
Ranking Skills

Now that you know the many skills required for running a business, take a close look at yourself. Which hats could you wear comfortably? Which will need adjusting? Use the stairway below to rank your business skills placing your strongest areas at the bottom of the stairway and your weakest ones towards the top.

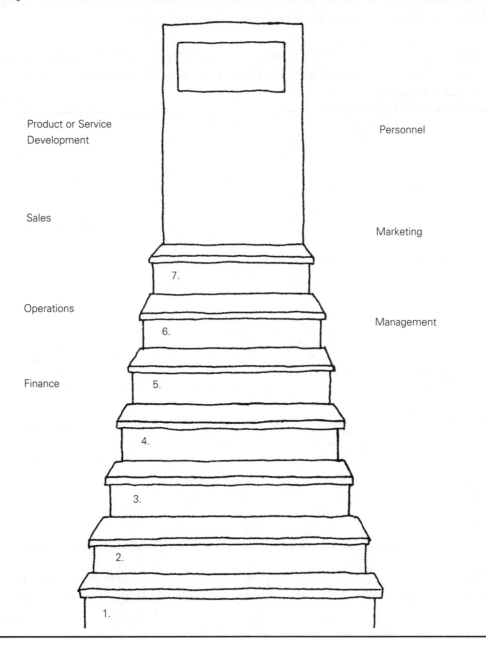

Product or Service Development

Personnel

Sales

Marketing

7.

Operations

Management

6.

Finance

5.

4.

3.

2.

1.

THE PURPOSE OF THIS WORKSHOP IS TO HELP YOU IDENTIFY AND CONTACT OUTSIDE RESOURCES FOR PURPOSES OF SELF-IMPROVEMENT

Personal Workshop #4
Getting Help

You have indicated in Personal Workshop #3 the skills you would like to acquire. Name at least two of those skills below. Then take action. How will you get help? Will you get a book from the library, attend a workshop, or make some phone calls? Use the resource list below to guide you as you plan to get help.

I Need Help With:

I Will Contact These Sources   **Notes**

_____

_____

_____

_____

_____

I Need Help With:

I Will Contact These Sources   **Notes**

_____

_____

_____

_____

_____

Personal Workshop #5
Risks & Rewards

Complete this workshop by listing as many risks and rewards as you can think of for the four categories listed. When you have completed your lists, review them. Which risks concern you the most? Think of ways you might be able to reduce those risks.

	Risks	Rewards
Career		
Family		
Psychological		
Financial		

You may want to make a copy of this workshop and have someone close to you complete it for you. When you are done, compare your findings. Share your results.

Personal Workshop #6
Financial Statements

Income

Look carefully at your current income, the income that you are used to living on. Your total income will probably go down somewhat during the first year of your business—but it may go down more than you expect if a significant part of your income is in the form of bonuses and commissions from your current job.

Annual Income	Amount ($)
Salary	
Bonuses & Commissions	
Rental Income	
Interest Income	
Dividend Income	
Capital Gains	
Partnership Income	
Other Investment Income	
Other Income (List)**	
Total Income	

Expenditures

Your current expenditures reflect your current income level. As income goes down, some expenses go down too—income taxes, both state and federal, for example, are based on what you actually earn. Look at this list carefully to see where you can whittle unnecessary expenses, and also look at those expenses which may go up. If you have benefited from employer-paid health insurance, will you now have to seek new coverage? At what cost to you?

Annual Expenditures	Amount ($)
Home Mortgage/Rental Payments	
Taxes	
State/Federal Income	
Real Estate	
Other	
Insurance	
Health	
Home Owner's	
Car	
Life	
Car Payments	
Other Loan Payments	
Telephone	
Gas/Electric Utilities	
Waste Disposal	
Alimony/Child Support	
Educational Expenses	
Medical/Dental Expenses	
Car Expense	
Food	
At Home	
Away from Home	
Clothing	
Household Operations/Supplies	
Recreation and Entertainment	
Savings and Investments	
Cash Contributions	
Other Expenses	
Total Expenditures	

Assets

Some assets can be used as **collateral** for loans or can be put into the business as part of your capital investment. Chairs and desks and bookcases, for example, can be used as office furniture; shop equipment from a hobby can be put to work making a product. This will vary from one business to another. Be as specific as you can with your list of personal property and "other assets."

AssetsAmount ($)	

Cash in the Bank
   (including money market
   accounts and CDs)	

Readily Marketable Securities	
Non-readily Marketable Securities	
Accounts and Notes Receivable	
Net Cash Surrender Value of Life Insurance	
Residential Real Estate	
Real Estate Investments	
Personal Property (Including Automobile)	
Other Assets (List:)	
A: Total Assets	

Liabilities

A list of your **liabilities** (what you owe) helps assess the strength of your collateral position. Assets you own free and clear are more likely to be acceptable to your banker than assets encumbered with debt. Note that some debts might be put on a different payment schedule, which in turn could lower your expenditures to a more comfortable level.

Liabilities	Amount($)
Notes Payable to the Bank	
Secured	
Unsecured	
Notes Payable to Others	
Secured	
Unsecured	
Accounts Payable (including credit cards)	
Margin Accounts	
Notes Due: Partnership	
Taxes Payable	
Mortgage Debt	
Life Insurance Loans	
Other Liabilities (list):	
Total Liabilities	
A: Total Assets	
B: Total Liabilities	
(A - B): Net Worth	
	$

Personal Workshop #7
Personal Goals

Write down your personal goals for the next year and for the next five years. Don't take a lot of time thinking about this. You can return to this workshop later and make changes. If you write down your goals you'll not only think about them more, you'll also take them more seriously.

Think of these goals as a work in progress. You'll develop other goals and interests and modify some of your initial goals. This first look gives you a basis on which to build.

My 5 Year Goals	Financial
	Family & Friends
	Social & Community
	Health & Fitness
	Personal Development
Goals for Next Year	Financial
	Family & Friends
	Social & Community
	Health & Fitness
	Personal Development

Personal Workshop #8
My Do and Don't List

What business do you see yourself in? What business don't you want to be in? List five businesses for each heading listed below. When you have completed your lists, look closely at your Do list. This list will help guide you as you continue to explore business ideas that are suitable for you.

Businesses

I DO Want to Be In: **I DON'T Want to Be In:**

1. _____   1. _____

_____   _____

2. _____   2. _____

_____   _____

3. _____   3. _____

_____   _____

4. _____   4. _____

_____   _____

5. _____   5. _____

_____   _____

THE PURPOSE OF THIS WORKSHOP IS TO VISUALIZE YOUR BUSINESS IN DETAIL

Personal Workshop #9
Visualizing My Business

As you visualize your business, think about the following questions:

- How much money are you earning? Be specific: "I'm earning $75, 000 a year" is more powerful than "Lots!"

- What kind of lifestyle are you and your family leading? Visualize in detail.

- How big is your business? (Dollar sales, outlets, employees, or other measures)

- How does your business reflect you and your values?

- What products and services are you offering?

- Imagine your customers. Who are they? How many? What are they like?

- Where is your business located?

- What does your place of business look like?

- Picture your employees. How many do you have? What are they doing? How are you treating them?

- What are you doing in the business? Do you like it?

Personal Workshop #10
Five Key Questions

1. What kind of **business** are you going to be in?	
2. What **industry** will you be in?	
3. What are your **products or services** going to be?	
4. Who will your **customers** be?	
5. What will be **special or distinctive** about your business?	

Personal Workshop #11
Going Shopping

Look for a business that is similar to the one you propose, one that sells the same products or services to the same kind of markets that you have chosen. The closer the match, the more useful this exercise will be.

List that business here:_____

Now "shop" this business as if you were their customer. Ask yourself what you like (and dislike) about the following areas:

	I Like:	I Dislike:
• product or service		
• courtesy		
• quality		
• location and appearance		
• prices		

If you were to take over this business, what would you do to make it better?

What areas need improving?

Now that you have had an opportunity to "shop" at a similar business, how will your business stand up to the competition? What is *your* competitive edge?

Personal Workshop #12
Weeding the Garden

A good business idea will stand out from a bad one as you "weed your garden." Circle yes or no in response to the questions below.

Does your business idea excite you?	Y	N
Can you see yourself running this business—and still smiling?	Y	N
Do you have experience in this kind of business?	Y	N
Do you have management experience?	Y	N
Do you have sales experience?	Y	N
Do you have experience in a related line of business?	Y	N
Do you have other experiences that might help in this business?	Y	N
Is the product or service well-defined and well-focused?	Y	N
Is there an apparent market demand for your products or service?	Y	N
Do you know how to reach that market?	Y	N
Will you have a competitive edge when you are in the market?	Y	N

Is the idea:

• simple?	Y	N
• personalized?	Y	N
• customized or specialized?	Y	N
Do you think you can afford to start such a business?	Y	N

Personal Workshop #13
Identify Your Industry Trends

Determine your SIC code. Look in the *Standard Industrial Classification Code Manual's* index to identify your business's 4-digit SIC code.

My **SIC** Code is:

Consult other reference books such as the *Encyclopedia of Associations* or *The Small Business Sourcebook*. These will steer you to the major trade associations and the major trade publications for your business.

My **national** trade association is:

    Their address and telephone number are:

My **regional** or local trade association is:

    Their address and telephone number are:

The most important **trade publications** for my industry are:

1.

2.

3.

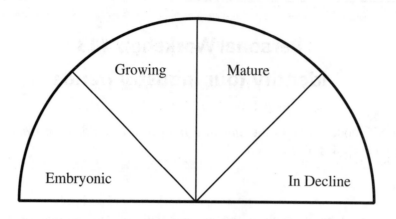

Industry Life Cycle

According to my trade association and trade publications, the major trends in my industry are:

a.   Place an X on the Life Cycle where your industry is today. Is it embryonic, growing, mature, or in decline?

b.   The **hot products** in this industry are:

c.   The **hot markets** for this industry are:

d.   Declining products and markets for this industry are:

THE PURPOSE OF THIS WORKSHOP IS TO IDENTIFY THE FEATURES AND BENEFITS OF YOUR PRODUCT OR SERVICE.

Personal Workshop #14

Features and Benefits
of My Product or Service

	Product or Service	Features	Benefits
1.			
2.			
3.			
4.			

THE PURPOSE OF THIS WORKSHOP IS TO DETERMINE WHO YOUR CUSTOMERS WILL BE, IF YOU WILL BE SELLING TO OTHER BUSINESSES OR ORGANIZATIONS INSTEAD OF (OR IN ADDITION TO) CONSUMERS.

Personal Workshop #15
Segmenting My Market—Consumer

Age (range)	
Sex (Male or Female)	
Income (range)	
Occupation	
Educational Level	
Home Address	
Lifestyle	
Etc.	

Segmenting My Market—Industrial

Standard Industrial Classification (SIC) code (4-digit preferred)

Geographic location, e.g., counties, metro areas, state, multi-state region, nation, multi-nation region, etc.

Size characteristics, e.g., annual sales volume, purchase volume, number of employees/production workers, number of establishments, etc.

Other variables, e.g., how product is used, buy class, service requirements, purchasing policies, and/or many others

Personal Workshop #16
Who Is My Competition?

Make a list of the competitors with whom you would be in direct competition. Then list those who would be considered indirect or potential competitors.

My direct competitors are:

1.

2.

3.

4.

5.

Other competitors (include indirect and potential competitors):

1.

2.

3.

4.

5.

THE PURPOSE OF THIS WORKSHOP IS TO LEARN MORE ABOUT YOUR COMPETITION

Personal Workshop #17
How Do My Competitors Compete?

Competitor:

Describe this competitor's:

Price

Service

Convenience

Location

Advertising

Other ways to compete (specify):

Personal Workshop #18
What Am I Going to Do About It?

Brainstorm to come up with competitive edge ideas. This should be fun to do as well as informative.

Try "The 10-Minute Solo Brainstorming Technique." Here's how it works:

Generate as many ideas as you can in a 10-minute period. Write them down, sketch them, talk into a tape recorder. Your goal is to generate ideas without editing or criticizing them. You want quantity. The more the merrier.

Now take some of your best (or wackiest) ideas and bounce them off your buddies. Which ideas might work? Which ones will you use to compete? Apply the basic brainstorming technique: the more ideas you can come up with, the better the chances that one or more will lead to a strong competitive edge

Personal Workshop #19

Estimated Start-Up Costs and Operating Budget

Part 1: List of Furniture, Fixtures, and Equipment

Leave out or add items to suit your business. Use separate sheets to list exactly what you need for each of the items below.	If you plan to pay cash in full, enter the full amount below and in the last column.	If you are going to pay by installments, enter in the down payment plus installments for 3 months.	Estimate of the cash you need for furniture, fixtures, and equipment.
Counters			
Storage shelves, cabinets			
Display stands, shelves, tables			
Cash register			
Computers and software			
Communications equipment (phone systems, fax)			
Copiers			
Safe			
Window display fixtures			
Special lighting			
Outside signage			
Delivery equipment			
Other (specify)			
Total: Furniture, Fixtures, Equipment. Enter under Part 1: Starting costs you only have to pay once.			

Part 2: Start-Up Costs You Only Have to Pay Once

Fixtures and equipment		XXXXXXXX	Put the total from Part 1 here
Decorating and remodeling		XXXXXXXX	Speak with contractor
Installation of fixtures and equipment		XXXXXXXX	Talk to suppliers from whom you buy these
Starting inventory		XXXXXXXX	Ask suppliers
Deposits for public utilities		XXXXXXXX	Ask utility companies
Legal and other professional fees		XXXXXXXX	Ask lawyer, accountant, etc.
Licenses and permits		XXXXXXXX	Find out from city offices
Advertising and promotion for opening		XXXXXXXX	Estimate: ask ad agencies
Accounts receivable		XXXXXXXX	What you will need to buy more stock until credit customers pay
Cash		XXXXXXXX	For unexpected expenses, losses, special purchases, etc.
Other (specify)		XXXXXXXX	Make a separate list and enter total
Total Estimated Cash you Need to Start:		XXXXXXXX	Add up all the numbers in column 1

Part 3: Operating Budget

Item	Monthly Expenses Column 1	Annual Expenses Column 2
Salary of owner or manager		
All other salaries and wages		
Rent or mortgage		
Advertising		
Delivery expense		
Supplies/materials		
Telephone/fax		
Utilities		
Insurance		
Taxes (Social Security only)		
Interest		
Loan payments		
Maintenance		
Professional Fees		
Miscellaneous		
Other (specify)		
Total Costs		

Personal Workshop #20
Is It Right for Me?

Does My Idea Make:

Personal Sense?	Yes	No
Business Sense?	Yes	No
Marketing Sense?	Yes	No
Financial Sense?	Yes	No

Index